T0360632

ROUTLEDGE LIBRARY EDITIONS:
MANAGEMENT

Volume 42

MANAGEMENT IN ACTION

MANAGEMENT IN ACTION

PETER LAWRENCE

Routledge
Taylor & Francis Group

LONDON AND NEW YORK

First published in 1984 by Routledge & Kegan Paul plc

This edition first published in 2018
by Routledge
4 Park Square, Milton Park, Abingdon, Oxon OX14 4RN
605 Third Avenue, New York, NY 10017

Routledge is an imprint of the Taylor & Francis Group, an informa business

British Library Cataloguing in Publication Data
A catalogue record for this book is available from the British Library

ISBN: 978-1-138-55938-7 (Set)
ISBN: 978-1-351-05538-3 (Set) (ebk)
ISBN: 978-0-8153-6533-4 (Volume 42) (hbk)
ISBN: 978-1-351-26172-2 (Volume 42) (ebk)

Publisher's Note
The publisher has gone to great lengths to ensure the quality of this reprint but points out that some imperfections in the original copies may be apparent.

Disclaimer
The publisher has made every effort to trace copyright holders and would welcome correspondence from those they have been unable to trace.

Peter Lawrence

Management
in Action

ROUTLEDGE & KEGAN PAUL
London, Boston, Melbourne and Henley

For *Vanessa Claire Lawrence*

First published in 1984
by Routledge & Kegan Paul plc

14 Leicester Square, London WC2H 7PH, England

9 Park Street, Boston, Mass. 02108, USA

464 St Kilda Road, Melbourne,
Victoria 3004, Australia and

Broadway House, Newtown Road,
Henley-on-Thames, Oxon RG9 1EN, England

Set in Press Roman
by Columns of Reading
and printed in Great Britain
by Billing & Sons Ltd, Worcester

ISBN 0-7100-9908-8

Contents

Preface

This is a book about what managers do, based largely on observation and experience. Like most attempts to describe something, it goes beyond simple description, by selecting, ordering and analysing. So that although it deals with the world and work of the manager as it is, rather than as it should be, it seeks to give some order to this by looking for patterns and connections, arranging material around themes, and putting it all together in a meaningful sequence.

There is already a substantial introductory literature on management, but many of these introductory books are about management systems and functions. They tend to depict the business company as a finely structured administrative machine, and its managers as computer-wise systems monitors. Such books tend to be formal and static, exhortatory and rather dry. They do not give a good idea of the way companies are actually run, or of what management work is really like. So there is scope for a book like this that tries to give a more life-like account of the realities of management, including the problems, crises and unresolved tensions.

Most writing about management is suffused with the idea that management is always and everywhere the same, that management work is governed by the same principles, has the same dynamics, and demands broadly similar skills from its practitioners. What is more, there are quite clearly several senses in which this is true. Management work invariably includes elements of planning, initiation and control, for example; there is generally a co-ordinative element; the ability to 'self-start' and motivate others is always important; social and political skills are usually central to the manager's ability to get things done; and so on. At the same time, recent research has shown that there is a lot of variety in terms of the pattern of activity and the content of management jobs. It makes a lot of difference whether one is talking about a salesman or a management accountant, about a manager in charge of a research unit or a factory, about a manager charged with buying raw materials for his company, or one whose work consists of devising manufacturing methods. So it is only fair to say what kind of managers are at the centre of this book.

This is primarily a study of production managers and general managers in charge of factories. It is not an attempt to say 'something about everything' on the subject of management, but to say a lot about managers concerned with the organisation of production and the direction of manufacturing concerns.

Production managers are a particularly good focus for insights into the reality of management for several reasons. First, production is a central activity, and one accounting for the bulk of a company's budget, workers and fixed assets. Second, production is very far from being an island, and has connections with a range of other departments and specialisms within the firm. This means that a study of production managers is a strategic site for the examination of the relations between various departments within a company. Third, there are more production managers than managers of any other kind, so to focus on their work is to be involved in the study of 'a major species'.

So our concern is with general and production managers, and most of the material is derived from a particular research project conducted by the author. This study was a three-part one involving a series of interviews with production managers, then a questionnaire survey, and finally a set of case studies in the form of periods spent as an observer of manufacturing operations in some thirty-five companies. It is the last of these, the observational case studies, which have yielded first-hand accounts of the work managers do, and some insight into why it is the way it is. There are two things to add.

The first is that this research was in two countries – Great Britain and West Germany – so there are managers of both nationalities in the sample, and the companies are not only located in the two countries, but by ownership are a mixture of British, American, German and Swiss. And of course the dual national base makes it possible to include some comparisons. It should be said that this book is not written in the form of a *systematic* comparison of British and German managers, and indeed the present writer has already written a book about German management.[1] But there are some occasions in the following chapters where it is helpful to point to Anglo-German differences, as for instance in the discussion of delivery punctuality, or interesting to identify practices as particularly British or German.

The second thing to add is that although a concern with general and production managers, based on the research project described, is at the centre of this book, there are some other sources to hand. In the last few years the present writer has made a study of technical managers in Germany, been associated with a comparative study of company organisation in France, interviewed a sample of purchasing managers in Britain, organised a study of British salesmen and sales managers, studied the workings of personnel departments in Germany, made a general study of industrial management in Sweden, and more generally been in and out of industry on a variety of assignments. The results of all this are secondary so far as the present book is concerned, but wherever there are gains of understanding or insight to be made by drawing from these other research studies, this is done.

The book is aimed primarily at management and business studies undergraduates in polytechnics and universities. Students who are committed to working in industry, and who have chosen a course of study oriented to that end, but who have not had much direct experience of industry yet, have most to gain from this book.

It is possible that older people doing post-experience courses, the Diploma in Management Studies, or MSc/MBA courses after industrial training, will also get something out of this book. Although they will know from experience most of what is presented here they may still benefit from having it presented systematically. Or to put it another way, they may enjoy the experience of having a mirror held up to the work of managers.

Lastly the book may be of help to students of sociology. Sociology degree courses invariably comprehend some component or option on industrial sociology. In this author's experience such courses owe their existence to a desire to explore questions interesting to the sociologist rather than to the wish to map the reality of industry and management for its own sake. This book may be a useful complement.

Note

1 Peter Lawrence, *Managers and Management in West Germany*, Croom Helm, 1980.

Acknowledgments

This book is based on a lot of contact with companies and managers in several countries, but especially in Great Britain and West Germany. Most of all I would like to thank these companies for their hospitality, and many managers for their readiness to talk to me about their work.

I would also like to thank my secretary Maxine Badcock at the University of Loughborough for her friendly and efficient work-processing of the manuscript.

1

What managers do all day

At 20.15 each evening in the summer Train 92 leaves Stockholm Central on a journey up through central-north Sweden, into the Arctic Circle, through Swedish Lapland, over the border to Norway, and finally along the fjord and into Narvik. Train 92 is popular with student holders of Euro-Railcards, and it goes as far north as one can get by train in western Europe. Indeed anyone who travels this line does have a feeling of having really got somewhere, until entering the town square in Narvik where a signpost tells by how many thousand kilometres you are still short of the North Pole. The first chapter is rather on this model. The intention really is to talk about 'what managers do all day', but this requires some hefty preliminaries to show how business firms are put together, who exactly production and general managers are, and where they fit in.

Sample organisation charts

A good way to propound the preliminaries is by means of example, using some organisation charts, but a word of warning is in order here. Textbooks often introduce charts or plans of organisation structure, but these are sometimes rather idealised, depicting a complete and perfect company organisation. This is a pity because an important point about company organisation structure is that there is a lot of variety.[1] There is, that is to say, a lot of variation about what the parts are, how they are put together, who or what reports to whom, and how it is depicted in the organisation chart. What is more, not all these differences can be explained rationally. While factors like the size of a company, what it requires to operate effectively, and in particular whether it 'stands alone' or is part of some larger corporate entity, are all important, there is still scope for personal choice, historical accident, pure empire building, and moulding jobs to management people. To try to get more out of the examples here we will use organisation charts from real companies in Britain or West Germany

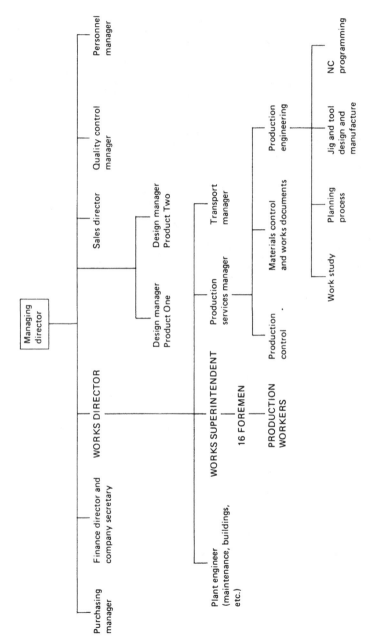

Figure 1.1   *British company making two types of industrial equipment, employing 450 people*

that have been studied in the research project on which the book is largely based. We will use more than one to get past the notion of a single 'one-best way', and try to footnote some of the differences and their causes.

A first view of company structure

The first challenge is this. To show who production managers are, one has to map the production function, and that is not easy or incontrovertible.

To make a start, consider the company depicted in Figure 1.1. It is a British company in the Midlands engaged in the manufacture of two industrial equipment products, sold both in Britain and abroad; it employs some 450 people.

Starting at the top, this company is headed by a managing director. This is not a truism: many companies, and still more particular works or factories, do not *legally* count as independent corporate entities, so the *de facto* chief executive will be called something else – works manager, plant manager, division manager, unit director and so on. Note also that of the eight managers on the next level down, from purchasing manager on the left to personnel manager on the right, some are directors and some are not. This may look organisationally messy, but it is not at all unusual. Whether or not a manager on this top line becomes a director will reflect various things, the general importance of his department to the particular company concerned, as well as the individual's personal merit, and an ingredient of pure chance.

Exploring this top line a little further a comment on purchasing, design, and quality control may be helpful. Most manufacturing companies have to buy raw materials, or much more likely, components, in order to make their products – hence a purchasing manager/purchasing section. In this case the purchasing manager reports direct to the managing director: this is normal with larger companies, and a recent survey by the British Institute of Management shows that it is becoming increasingly common.[2] But it does not have to be this way, indeed it is quite common for the purchasing function to come under production and report to a works director or higher production manager.

Not all companies have a research and development capability: R & D tends to be a feature of large companies, and ones whose product or service is technically sophisticated. Rather more companies have a design function, as with the company depicted in Figure 1.1, and having a design department goes further down the size scale of companies. The importance of design also varies from company to company. At the strong end, creative design, perhaps responding to refined customer need or incorporating the rising high-water mark of a developing technology, will be the very essence of a company's business, without which it will achieve nothing. The aircraft industry is a good example. In such cases design will be represented at board of directors level in the person of a technical or engineering director. In the case of the company shown in Figure 1.1 design is not that important. At any point in time the company has designed products, in manufacture, for sale. On the other hand, there is scope for improving the models, and one of the two basic products can be made in a variety of ways, and the design and the manufacturing method are related. What is more this same basic product can be made in all sorts of shapes and sizes to suit customer needs, but the particular customer need may require an input from design in the first place. So in this case a design department exists, or rather two parallel design sections for each of the two basic products, but is not important enough to rate board status. And of course there are other companies too small to have a design capability at all, or whose product is so simple and unchanging for design not to be an issue.

It is also often the case that some particular factory or works will not have a design section because this design capability is located elsewhere. There are many American-owned machine tool companies in Britain, for example, where the design and development work is mostly done in the USA, and then these machine tools of American design are actually manufactured in factories in Britain. Even where there is no separation by national ownership there is a tendency to separate R & D establishments and design centres geographically; in Britain they are often located in choice country houses far from the grime of manufacturing sites. And with multi-national companies this separation of design/R & D may reach international proportions: the Swedish mining equipment corporation Atlas Copco, for example, whose head office and main works are in Stockholm, has its R & D centre in French-speaking Switzerland.

Finally, with regard to the top line in Figure 1.1, note the position of the quality control manager. A company would have to be much larger than that depicted in Figure 1.1 for the quality control manager to be a full director (or the product would have to be very critical from a safety point of view) but it is still normal to have the head of the quality control or inspection department report directly to the managing director or other most senior person on site. The intention here is quite simply to guarantee the independence of judgments about quality by protecting inspectors from interference by production bosses or anyone else. This splendid principle may get modified in practice in two ways. First, in very small companies inspection may in fact come under the control of production; it may be difficult to avoid this in a company so small that there is only one level of management between the foreman and the owner-manager. Second, it is not unusual for a production manager to control the inspectors with regard to the allocation of work and priorities, while they report to an independent quality control manager with regard to standards (and it is even more common for production managers to work towards a situation like this unofficially).

Moving to the next level down, that of the four direct subordinates of the works director, the plant engineer on the left is in charge of the repair and maintenance of the buildings and machinery. Companies invariably have some person or section in charge of maintenance, but its importance varies. The maintenance function tends to be most important in assembly-line mass production factories working shifts, such as car factories, and in process industry plants with near continuous production, such as the chemical works and food processing companies. It is common for maintenance to come under the control of a higher production manager, as in the company shown in Figure 1.1, but it does not have to be this way. Maintenance may be entirely separate from production, reporting directly to the managing director, or the maintenance team may report to a technical or engineering director who is separate from the works or production director. Where maintenance is separate it often gives rise to complaints by production managers that the maintenance service is inadequate (e.g. too slow, shows too little sense of urgency), with maintenance managers making counter-claims that production workers abuse the equipment while their bosses lack any appreciation of the problems of maintenance.

The works superintendent, the next manager on this line, is of course a part of the production chain of command. He has some sixteen foremen reporting to him, who in turn supervise teams of production workers. Superintendent is a common name for this rank in the production hierarchy immediately above the foreman level, but it is not invariable. Part of the natural variation referred to at the start of the chapter is that there are few standardised job titles or ranks in industry, and that is equally true for Germany as for Britain.

Moving again to the right the three functions of production control, materials control, and production engineering are all grouped under the production services manager. This is a neat organisational arrangement. The purpose of the production control section is to devise and monitor a production schedule: to decide, that is, what manufacturing jobs are to be done in what order to what deadlines, and then to try to see the schedule is adhered to. The production control function is most important (and intricate) in a company which is making a lot of different things in different quantities, for separate customers expecting delivery at different times. It is least important in process industry plants running more or less continuously with the plant having a controlled variable output. In these cases it is more a matter of production planning, of deciding how much is needed in a time period and adjusting plant output accordingly.

The materials control section is concerned with lining up things the company has bought (raw materials, bought-out-parts) ready for their use in production, and keeping tabs on them. Materials control is not always a separate organisational entity as in the company depicted in Figure 1.1. Sometimes it is comprehended by production control. And sometimes production control and purchasing are joined organisationally, on the grounds that the schedule will depend on the availability of the parts and materials bought by the purchasing section so that the two activities need to be integrated. And to complete the variety scenario, materials control often appears on a company organisation chart as an umbrella for purchasing and production control – especially in German companies.

Moving again to the right, production engineering is broadly speaking a link between design and production. Designers will produce a model of a new product, or newly modified product, but they will not tell anyone how to make it. This is done by production engineering, who will devise manufacturing methods, solve technical problems relating to manufacture, and generally assist in the process of production. In the company depicted in Figure 1.1 production engineering is broken down into sub-sections. The work study section will time jobs and part jobs with a view to establishing payment rates for the workers who do them. Planning process is concerned with detailing a sequence of operations to complete various jobs. The jig and tool section will make up any tools or other appliances that are needed on the shop floor to help to make the company's products. And the NC programming section prepares and edits the tapes used to run numerically controlled machines in the workshop.

Production engineering, materials control and production control are not always grouped under a production services manager. In many companies they would appear separately at the works superintendent level (or higher). Finally with reference to Figure 1.1, the works director's last subordinate is the transport manager. One of the products produced by this company is consumed in a routine way by other firms so that some scheduled deliveries take place; this is what is organised by the transport manager. Not all companies have a transport section of course. Some leave their customers to collect the goods, others hire hauliers to do the deliveries for them. On the other hand some consumer goods companies, especially if they serve a chain of retail outlets (breweries, for instance) will have an elaborate distribution system which will figure prominently on the organisation chart.

The company depicted in Figure 1.1 was chosen deliberately because its operations are technically quite detailed and thus give an opportunity to explain a range of interlocking parts. At the same time, the organisational arrangements of this company have been used for relativising purposes, to indicate how things might be different elsewhere. This leads to a new question, that of identifying the production managers.

Who are the production managers?

There are two answers to this apparently straightforward question, and again we may take Figure 1.1 as a starting point. One view would be that the works director and all those of managerial rank directly or indirectly reporting to him are production managers. After all, they are all doing things closely allied to production, as has been made clear in the previous section. The other view is that the real production managers are those forming a direct line from the top to the production workers at the bottom, this line being denoted in capitals in Figure 1.1. So that in this company there are only two production managers in the strong sense: the works superintendent, who is solely concerned with direct manufacture, and the works director, whose responsibilities importantly include direct manufacture.

It is the second of these views which is preferred here. Production managers are those who are responsible for *direct* manufacture, some of them being responsible for related activities as well. But managers solely in charge of related activities – the production controllers, purchasing managers, production engineers, materials controllers, maintenance managers, and so on – are excluded. So the sample of production managers whose work is reported here are production managers in the strong and narrow sense. The manufacturing manager shown in Figure 1.2 is a good example.

The company shown in Figure 1.2 is a consumer goods company in West Germany employing some 350 people. The manufacturing manager in this company is solely responsible for direct manufacture. His immediate

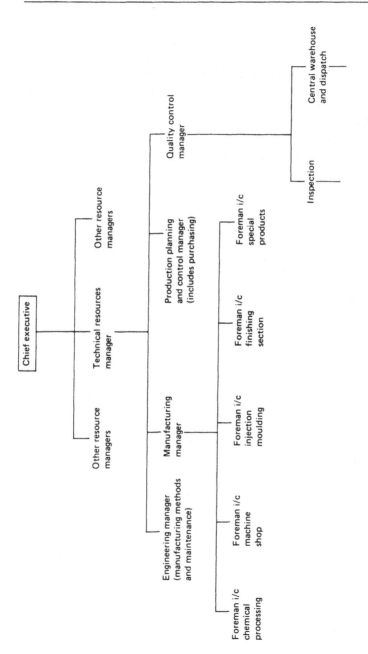

Figure 1.2 *Company in West Germany making consumer goods, 350 employees*

subordinates are five foremen in turn in charge of various production operations. This manager is assisted at his own level by an engineering manager responsible for both manufacturing methods and maintenance, and by a production planning and control manager whose responsibilities include the purchase of necessary parts and materials. The quality control manager is responsible for the warehouse and dispatch of finished goods as well as for inspection. Like so many of these arrangements, it makes good sense but it does not have to be like this.

It should be added in connection with this example that the span of control of the German foreman tends to be larger than that of his opposite number in Britain; the German foreman, that is, tends to supervise a larger number of production workers. The German foreman is also often qualified in a formal way, as well as by experience and character.[3] These two facts make the German foreman a more consequential figure in the company organisation, both more opinionated and capable of taking on more. In this particular company, for example, the foremen made recommendations about capital equipment purchase, assisted the manufacturing manager in quality tests and calculations, visited other companies to inspect machinery, and occasionally visited the sister company in northern Spain to advise on operations.

General managers

The sample of observed managers whose work is discussed include some general managers. By general manager is meant a manager who is responsible for a range of functions, not just production and its closely related activities, or a manager who is in charge of a complete manufacturing works or unit, not just the direct manufacturing operation therein. An example of such a general manager in the sample, one who in fact fits both criteria, is the works director of the company depicted in Figure 1.3. This is a food processing company in West Germany, employing some 550 people.

This manager is in charge of a complete manufacturing unit, which in turn is just one of many works making up the nation-wide company with its national headquarters on another site. This of course explains the omissions: sales, market research, R & D, corporate policy, and so on, are being done at head office or at separate establishments. Nevertheless, the works director at this company is in charge not only of production planning, production, quality control, and maintenance — the hard-line production-related functions — but also of personnel, buying, administration and safety.

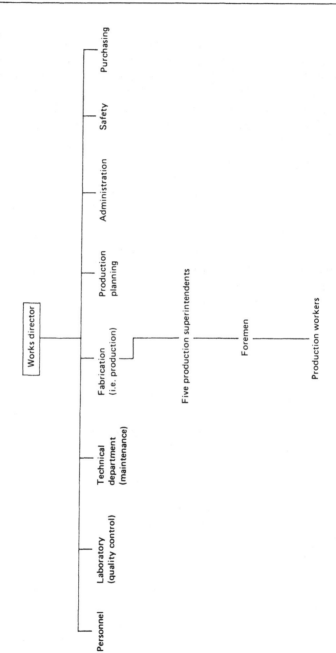

Figure 1.3 *Food processing company in West Germany, with 550 employees*

Big companies which are broken down into a number of separate, more or less independent works, each with its own head, a kind of on-site chief executive, tend to strengthen the production hierarchy. Being the head of such a works is an important position and manifestation of career success; the way to it is typically up the production hierarchy. The fabrication manager at this company, a PhD incidentally, is a good example. He was absent at the time of the study on a course in England to improve his English before going on a nine-month course at an international business school prior to promotion.

Note that quality control at this company is in the form of a laboratory and its staff. This is typical of the food processing industry, where quality control is not a matter of mechanical tests of completed products but of continually monitoring a process and sampling 'the product' at various stages in that process. We suggested earlier that it is production planning rather than production control which is appropriate in the process industry: this is borne out in the case of the company, where adjusting the output of the plant to the demand for the produce is the necessary operation.

A blurred distinction

So far we have spoken of a sample made up of production managers and general managers, defined both and given examples. But the distinction is not always so sharp, especially where the size of the organisation increases. Consider, for instance, the manufacturing director in the company depicted in Figure 1.4. It is a British company in the south-east making specialist machinery and employing some 700 people.

According to the criteria, the manufacturing director is a production manager rather than a general manager, yet his responsibilities are obviously considerable. He has (slightly) more managerial subordinates than the managing director, the machine shop is of a size to require sub-division between two superintendents and there is a separate assembly section, and the manufacturing director is at the top of a production hierarchy with five levels between the production workers and the managing director. What is more he acts as the managing director's deputy during the latter's frequent absences abroad. The holistic nature of his responsibility for production and all that goes with it is highlighted by comparison with the sales function. Even at board level the sales operation is sub-divided both by region and by major and minor products.

We have introduced this last example just to show that so much in management work is relative. Not only is there no standard (and certainly

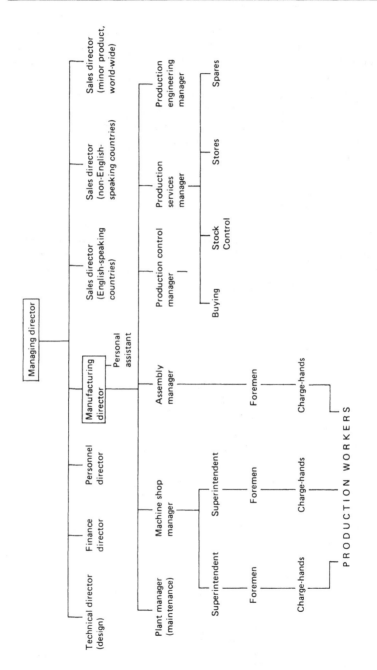

Figure 1.4 *British company making specialist machinery, employing 700 people*

no one best) organisation structure for companies; but by juxtaposing different companies one can cast doubt on a commonly accepted distinction such as that between general and functional managers.

Classifying management work

Most management work is active not contemplative. There are a few specialist management jobs which involve a lot of working alone, thinking, analysing, calculating and writing — jobs in financial control, management services, some specialist technical work, and so on — but these are a minority. The work of most managers is active, and interactive. The simplest answer to the question of what managers do all day, is that they go to meetings, and talk to people. So any classification scheme for management work, any typology of executive activity, must take account of the strongly interactive nature of management work and must make some sense of it.

The particular challenge in reporting the work that managers do is to make some order out of the endless series of meetings, talks and contacts, or one will end up with a statement along the lines of 'managers spend some three-quarters of their time talking to people in one way or another'. While true, such a statement is too generalised to be of much help. What is needed is an attempt to make this body of interactive work intelligible by categorising it as to form, giving examples of the main types and providing an elucidatory commentary on some of the activities. Our study of forty-one general managers and production managers in thirty-six companies in Britain and West Germany suggests the following scheme.

A typology for the interactive manager

Since managers spend much time at meetings and in other purposeful contacts, the first need is to break this down into some more manageable categories, and we suggest the three following:

1a   Time spent in formal, *recurrent scheduled meetings*. By a formal meeting we refer to the form and setting in the sense of the meeting having a defined beginning and end, with delegates probably sitting round a table, possibly with a written agenda, and with interruptions kept to a minimum. By scheduled we mean that the meeting is fixed in advance, not immediately prior to its commencement; by recurrent we mean that these are meetings which occur regularly, usually at fixed intervals, and often at the same time and place. This designation of formal recurrent scheduled meetings covers such types as the daily (usually twice daily in the motor car industry) production progress meetings, weekly production planning meetings, regular meetings about the supply of purchased parts and materials, monthly departmental meetings chaired by general managers (or senior production managers) of a general purpose kind.

1b   Time spent in *convened special purpose meetings*. Like the meetings referred to in 1a above, these are also formal and usually involve more than two participants. The time and place of such meetings may be arranged well in advance, or immediately prior to the meeting, and the former is more usual. The key difference between the convened meeting and the scheduled recurrent meeting is that the former is not recurrent at fixed intervals. This convened special purpose meeting category covers such actual examples as meetings with sales and export managers about particular orders, with shop stewards and convenors in response to employee grievances, with production engineers about methods problems, with maintenance managers about the process of repairs, and so on.

1c   Refers to *ad hoc discussions*. First, these are not recurrent in the sense that the participants meet regularly *for the same purpose* even if they meet frequently for various purposes. With regard to the subject matter of the discussion they are 'one-off' meetings. Second, they typically involve only two people; meetings of more than two people are usually more formal and are classified under 1a or 1b above. Third, these *ad hoc* discussions are normally not arranged in advance but are set up by means of an 'are you free' or 'can I come over for ten minutes' type phone call; sometimes the time and place of the meeting is practically left to chance. This heading of *ad hoc* discussions includes a range of one-to-one meetings with all types of subordinates, superiors and same rank colleagues. These *ad hoc* discussions are more numerous than either the formal recurrent meetings or the convened special purpose meetings; or more precisely, these *ad hoc* discussions account for a higher proportion of the manager's time than either of the two types of formal meetings, and that is particularly true for German managers. These three categories give us a way of breaking down the range of meetings and discussions, and in the next chapter we will elaborate on the subject matter and topics, and give examples. Next we need a category for time spent in the works, on the shop floor.

2   Time spent *in the works*. That managers spend some time on the shop floor or making tours of the works is not a truism. After all, even production managers do not actually work the machines themselves, nor do they directly supervise workers; their foremen do this. Yet most

production managers do spend a significant amount of time on the shop floor, some general managers do, and even most chief executives say it is a good idea to do so even if they do not find the time to do so as often as they would like. In the next chapter we will take up the question of exactly what ends are served by these tours of the works, but broadly speaking it is an opportunity for managers to show their face, greet workers and colleagues, pass on instructions and information, gather impressions, check what is happening, and exercise general surveillance. These tours of the works are frequently rather chatty affairs, with greetings and snappy instructions alternating with *ad hoc* discussions of the 1c type. Indeed the tour of the works might be parodied as 'the continuation of meetings by other means'. This is also true of the use of the telephone, which deserves a category of its own.

3   Time spent *on the telephone*. The extent to which managers use the telephone for either internal (works) calls or external ones varies a great deal. But if one averages out the time spent telephoning by a group of managers it emerges as a significant minority time activity – and it is not far short of the time spent on all kinds of office work. What is more, telephoning is different in kind from the other forms of communication – meetings, *ad hoc* discussions and little chats in the course of touring the works. It is generally limited to two parties (few European managers yet have the equipment for teleconferences), it links the initiator with people who are not physically present and in the case of external calls people who could not otherwise be made available, and of course incoming calls structure time use because they have to be responded to as they occur.

4   *Office work*. Although management work is primarily interactive managers do spend some time working in their offices, and we need a category for this. So the office work category refers to time the manager spends working at his or her own desk, either alone or accompanied only by a secretary (or occasionally a personal assistant). This category covers such activities as correspondence, report writing, absorbing information and preparing for meetings.

5   The final category is an artificial but necessary one. The very act of carrying out a study may affect the results, so that it is desirable to try to control for this. If, for example, one attempts to find out how managers spend their time by getting them to fill in activity diaries (this has been the commonest method) then logically there ought to be a category for time spent filling in the diary. In the present study where observation has been the principal method it is even more important to check since inevitably the manager and observer will come into conversation and indeed the

observer actually needs some commentary and explanation to make sense of all that is going on. So our last category is for time spent *giving explanations to the observer*.

So this in brief, is the typology:

1a Formal scheduled recurrent meetings — several participants.
1b Convened special purpose meetings — generally several participants.
1c *Ad hoc* discussions — usually only two participants.
2 Tours of the works, time spent in the works.
3 Telephoning.
4 Office or desk work.
5 Explanations to researcher.

With this scheme we can examine how samples of British and German managers spent several working days.

German managers at work

We first tried out the scheme on sixteen German managers with the results shown in Table 1.1.

Table 1.1

Activity type		Proportion of observed time spent on it (%)
1a	Formal scheduled recurrent meetings	9.78
1b	Convened special purpose meetings	12.62
1c	*Ad hoc* discussions	20.07
2	Time spent in the works	16.87
3	Telephoning	10.66
4	Office work	11.56
5	Explanations	10.45
Total time accounted for		91.98

It will be seen straight away that this categorising scheme passes the acid test — it works. The seven categories, six of them real and one an artificial control, serve to cover over 90 per cent of the working time of a group of German managers.

The remaining 8 per cent of time not accounted for can be explained in two ways. First, it is made up of occasional one-off activities, not repeated by the individual concerned or replicated by any other manager in the study. One of the managers, for example, spent some time getting equipment out of a snowdrift, another drew dollars out the bank for a business trip to the USA, and so on. Second, there is a residue of dead time, of time which is not meaningfully or constructively spent, and which it is therefore pointless to categorise. Under this second heading come things such as waiting for visitors, waiting to see people, waiting for meetings to start. There will always be a residual element of dead time no matter what categorisation scheme is used.

It is also fair to speculate as to how the 10 per cent of time spent giving explanations to the observer would normally have been used, and again there are two answers. Some of that time would probably have been spent on office work: there was an observable tendency for managers to use the study as a reason to postpone desk work and get on with something active. The second answer is that some of the time would probably have been spent in more *ad hoc* discussions. Again it was observable that casual callers on a manager would tend to go away if the manager had someone else around.

British managers at work

The scheme also comprehends quite nicely the work of a larger sample of twenty-five British managers, as is shown in Table 1.2.

Table 1.2

Activity type		*Proportion of observed time spent on it (%)*
1a	Formal scheduled recurrent meetings	15.50
1b	Convened special purpose meetings	14.46
1c	*Ad hoc* discussions	17.93
2	Time spent in works	17.35
3	Telephoning	7.23
4	Office work	11.16
5	Explanations	12.08
Total time accounted for		95.92

The scheme fits British managers even better in fact, and it is clear that the first two categories, for the two types of formal meeting, are even more relevant to the analysis of the work of managers in Britain. Apart from this difference with regard to time spent on formal meetings, the similarities are quite striking. Whatever differences there may be between the style or *modus operandi* of British and German managers, they do not show up in analysis of the distribution of working time between broad classes of activities.

Management work: an overview

We have already reached the point where a number of generalisations can be made about the nature of management work. It is highly interactive. Claims that management is 'all about communication' clearly have some substance. So does the textbook formula that management is about getting things done with or through other people. The amount of time spent on office work is relatively small; indeed a manager will actually spend little time in his own office unless he is receiving visitors or holding meetings there.

This interaction, this contact with others, takes place in a number of ways ranging from formal meetings through less formal *ad hoc* discussions to telephone conversations and brief exchanges while touring the works. It is also clear that one can break down the idea of meetings by grading them in terms of formality, number of participants, venue and mode of scheduling, as well as by the more obvious method of topic and subject. Both production managers and general managers tend to spend time on the shop floor or going round the works even though most of them do not strictly speaking have to. Furthermore these findings are broadly similar for managers in both Britain and West Germany.

The next stage, to be pursued in Chapter 2, is clearly to examine more closely the content of activities recorded under these general headings.

Summary

We have argued that there is some variation in the way that companies are put together and organisationally structured, and sought to illustrate this contention using several organisation charts depicting companies in Britain and Germany. At the same time we used this exercise to show what is meant by production managers and general managers, and to show how they fit into the company structure. To assist a background understanding, especially of the work of production managers, we explained briefly the work of contingent functions in industry including production control, materials control, purchasing, maintenance, production engineering and quality control. Having then elaborated a scheme for classifying the observable work of managers in terms of various types of meeting, office work, telephoning and tours of the works, we successfully applied this scheme to groups of managers in Britain and Germany as a preliminary to a more detailed discussion of these activities.

Notes

1 For a more detailed discussion of the notion of variations in company structure, see P.A. Lawrence and R.A. Lee, *Insight into Management*, Oxford University Press, 1984, Chapter 2.
2 A report by the British Institute of Management shows that in more and more companies the purchasing function is becoming independent in the sense of reporting to a purchasing director or direct to the chief executive. See Brian Farrington and Michael Woodmansey, *The Purchasing Function*, Management Survey Report no. 50, British Institute of Management, 1980.
3 For a more detailed treatment of the differences in training and status between British and German foremen, see Peter Lawrence, *Managers and Management in West Germany*, Croom Helm, 1980, Chapter 7.

Further reading

Suggestions for further reading relating to the ideas explored in the first two chapters will be given at the end of Chapter 2.

Discussion questions

Questions for discussion relating to the first two chapters will also appear at the end of Chapter 2.

2

The content of management work

There is an entertaining John Cleese film called *Meetings Bloody Meetings* which is used for management training. Some of the clips show a production manager conducting uproariously chaotic meetings where the members are all at cross purposes and united only by their resentment of the chairman. The film makes very well the point that meetings need proper preparation, time budgeting, and a system of priorities, but often do not have the benefit of these. It is only fair to show the other side of the picture, to indicate what it is that renders the meetings which managers take part in such a challenge. It is really two related things. First, there is the sheer volume of information which managers exchange with each other and monitor; and second, there is range and diversity of issues which require some decision, control or co-ordination. We will illustrate some of this diversity by taking a closer look at the various categories of meetings and discussions outlined in the last chapter.

Scheduled recurrent meetings

These are the formal meetings (type 1a from the last chapter) which are planned in advance and recur, usually at fixed intervals. As a first example, consider the daily fare of a senior production manager in a car factory in Britain. This manager is three levels above the foreman, two down from the chief executive, and has eight production superintendents as his direct subordinates.

1 He usually chairs two meetings with his eight superintendents each day, mid-morning and mid-afternoon. They are general purpose meetings where the group reviews everything that has happened since the last meeting (a few hours earlier) and looks at the problems of the immediate future. This is the most basic and widespread kind of recurrent meeting for production managers – only the frequency varies. These meetings will be concerned with shortages and stoppages, manning and work distribution,

technical and quality issues and, above all, deadlines and output.

2 This manager goes to a daily display cum meeting run by the head of quality control. The form of this meeting is that eight or ten cars will have been picked at random from the previous few hours' production, inspected rigorously and then put on display with their defects highlighted. Production managers swarm over the display feeling variously guilty, resentful or unconcerned, and the proceedings are topped off with a snappy address from the quality control boss.

3 The production manager chairs an additional meeting with his superintendents each week to decide on the level of overtime working required each weekend.

4 The manager also attends a daily meeting chaired by the chief executive or his deputy and attended by all the senior managers. Like the production manager's meeting with his superintendents, these are general purpose meetings, even more wide-ranging, though the time span for most of the issues is short. Mass production industry in general, and the automobile industry in particular, are marked by a pervasive sense of urgency and pressure. To give a small indicator, at this company the chief executive has in his office a digital clock showing the number of cars made since the start of the working day – they make getting on for 1,000 per twenty-four-hour period, so the clock actually 'ticks over'.

Let us take as a second example a senior production manager in a fork lift truck factory in south Germany. This manager has only one scheduled recurrent meeting per week, but it lasts a whole day. It is called the *Termingespräch* (lit. deadline discussion), what would be a production control meeting in England, where this manager's team go through their complete job list, check that everything is on schedule, and take action if any job is running late. In fact, at the meeting we attended, nothing was running late, and those present brought forward the deadlines for some additional jobs to give themselves a challenge.

As a third example we will take a production manager at a factory in Wales making steel tubes. In the short period of the study this manager attended two scheduled recurrent meetings. The first a production control meeting like that described in the previous German example, though of more modest proportions (i.e. it lasted 1½ hours, and takes place monthly). This meeting was chaired by the production control manager, and attended by his subordinates, the production manager, and the appropriate salesman, and was in the form of the salesman being informed of completed or expected batches of tubes and in turn in-putting new orders. The second of the scheduled meetings attended by the manager is something new, namely a shop committee meeting. Although there is no *system* of industrial democracy in Britain, as there is, for example, in West Germany, Sweden, Norway and some of the Eastern Bloc countries, still many firms have created some committees where workers' representatives and management meet to discuss common interests, and do so in a routine (scheduled recurrent!) way, not just in response to some crisis. The works committee meeting which this manager chaired is of this kind, and is a monthly occurrence. Members of the general public brought up on media alarmism might be surprised by the co-operative nature of such committees on many occasions. This particular one began with the production manager reading out a personal message from the managing director congratulating a major division of the works on the highest ever output.

We could give many more examples but it would not add to the basic pattern. This is that there are three basic types of recurrent meetings for production and general managers, the first two of which overlap:

1 *Production meetings* in a narrow and immediate sense, concerned with supplies (of parts and materials), manning and, above all, deadlines and output.

2 *Departmental meetings* held by general or senior production managers, usually at longer time intervals, attended by all their immediate subordinates. These departmental meetings are general purpose, more wide ranging than the production meetings, and have a longer time scale. We will give an example in a moment.

3 *Employee-representative committees* like the one referred to in the case of the production manager at the steel tubes factory above. Most British companies of any size have some kind of a worker-management liaison committee, and these are usually chaired by a production manager and sometimes by the most senior manager on site.

The important thing at this stage is to look at one or two of these departmental meetings and see the sort of issues that may arise.

Departmental meetings

As a first example we will take the weekly meeting of a general manager in charge of a heavy fabrications unit in the Midlands. This unit counts as one of the company's six manufacturing divisions but it is on a separate site, which gives the general manager a lot of independence. Most of the work of this unit is subcontract work for the other five divisions, but they do some work for direct customers. The meeting is attended by the general manager's immediate subordinates: the works accountant, the production superintendent, the chief production engineer, the materials controller, the chief buyer and the head of quality control. This is not 'big business'; the unit employs 160 people. These are some of the issues discussed at a sample meeting:

1 First, the general manager passes on a miscellany of information he obtained at an earlier meeting of the heads of manufacturing divisions chaired by one of the directors – a trade fair coming to the area and delegates to visit the company; press visitors coming to the unit (it has not been open long); company about to mount a study of its computer needs; the company newspaper is coming out a month late; someone is devising drill for bomb scare emergencies; all grades of workers at the company have just received the company's offers of wage rises (and most have rejected them!); and holiday forms for employees to complete are handed out.

2 Discussion of the (high) level of stock which the general manager is trying to reduce; the stock level is artificially high because the unit is holding materials for work for another of the divisions but the order has not actually been placed.

3 The chief buyer is to take up with the post office complaints about the telephones.

4 General discussion of the orders for products.

5 Related discussion on how to overcome a bottleneck in the unit: the general manager urges them to sort it out and aim for £2,000,000 worth of completed work by the (imminent) end of the financial year.

6 The works accountant asks to have the office windows cleaned.

7 The general manager reports a case in another division where a manager stopped an employee half a day's pay for absence, and tells his team he does not want them to stoop to such pettiness.

8 The works accountant reports an 18 per cent rise in the unit's output in the previous month.

9 The accountant also congratulates the team on the efficient way the recent stock-taking exercise was carried out, but informs them that various items are missing.

10 This last point leads to a discussion of possible explanations of these missing materials: they are being stolen by workers, or the night shift, or taken by maintenance without permission, or maybe legitimately transferred to other divisions but the authorisation forms have been lost.

11 At this juncture the general manager receives a phone call from the main works to say that tool-room and maintenance workers (those belonging to the engineering workers union, the AEUW) have gone on strike to

register their displeasure at the inadequate pay offer. He passes this on to the meeting.

12 The materials controller and general manager discuss their expected co-operation with a neighbouring (larger) firm, doing subcontract work for them.

13 The production superintendent reports various machinery breakdowns and asks for action.

14 The superintendent also reports an employee wages grievance: the direct workers (production workers) think the indirect workers (clerks, inspectors, maintenance people) are getting a bonus based on the output of the direct workers, and are resentful. It is not true, but the general manager agrees to straighten them out.

15 Finally, the general manager gives a progress report on the building work; business is expanding fast, and the unit is being enlarged.

The first impression is probably that the meetings handle a lot of little things. It is true that the variety of issues is considerable — orders, breakdowns, housekeeping, relations with the main works, strike, telephone defects, stock-taking, employee grievances and so on. But it is also important to register that a few of the issues are in fact very important. The order situation, bottleneck problems, and relations with the neighbouring firm, are all quite critical for the unit's expansion.

We will take the next example from a much bigger company, a large German electronics firm. This time it is the monthly meeting held by a senior production manager in charge of one of the company's product divisions. There are still some local and homely issues, but there is also a general scaling-up, and some new dimensions. The meeting is attended by the divisional manager's four immediate subordinates in charge of manufacturing, production control, engineering and quality control.

1 The quality control manager is asked how fast he can process (have inspected) a big job being exported to China: they discuss the mechanics of this.

2 The divisional manager takes up with the production control manager some part of this same export order which is running late.

3 The company has a wire-winding section whose existence and purpose is being challenged by the company head office (in another city). The group get together to defend this section against head office attack by marshalling relevant arguments — it makes components for the rest of the works, its productivity is rising steadily, and so on.

4 This leads them into a wider discussion of how the composition of the workforce should conform to the needs of the division not to some

abstract formula (supplied by head office!).

5 The divisional manager asks the group for their first reaction to the possibility of buying some new machines. They respond enthusiastically and plunge straight away into a discussion of the technical specifications, and later of the delivery times quoted by suppliers.

6 The chairman complains about maintenance costs, and the team are encouraged to reduce them.

7 They discuss provisional arrangements for a big order they are hoping to get for Brazil, in particular how much of the work can be done in Germany and how much on site in Brazil.

8 They discuss piece work rates in the paint shop, and the chairman asks if the engineering manager who is responsible for this rate setting will be able to 'sell' these rates to the Works Council (the employee representative committee mandatory in German firms).

9 The chairman announces the retirement of a colleague due to ill health, and they discuss his replacement. The critical point is that this colleague works in a no-man's-land area between engineering and development; development reports to a different manager, and the group want a replacement who will be part of their team exclusively. It is agreed that the engineering manager will lobby to this effect and the others will back him up.

10 It is mid-November and at the end the chairman reminds the group that, although it has lapsed recently, the managers used to have a night out with the workers before Christmas. They agree to do this, and have an eager discussion of pubs and restaurants. As a follow-up, one of the managers speaks of the difficulty of working normally on the three days between Christmas and New Year if employees take extra time off. The divisional manager declines to close the works for this period.

Note that in this case the time scale has lengthened: equipment to be purchased months later is discussed, arrangements for an order they expect but have not got yet, even post-Christmas working arrangements in mid-November. There is a similar up-grading of the orders and deadlines issues that come up for discussion – heavy-weight export orders to China and Brazil. A new element is the obvious feuding with head office – over justifying some special section, and at a more general level over personnel policy. It is a fact of corporate life that head office directives are generally resented. Nothing induces loyalty in a group of managers like a head office initiative they wish to frustrate. The above meeting also exhibits some rather German features, most obviously the concern with machinery purchase. It is difficult to spend a couple of days in a German firm without someone somewhere wanting to spend a million DM on equipment purchase. The divisional manager's refusal to close the works for the three (doubtless undermanned) days between Christmas and New Year is also in our experience quite typical: German managers are not such ready compromisers.

There is one particular type of meeting which we have not covered so far in this discussion of formal meetings and this is the occasion on which a manager reports to his superior. Although only two people are involved, such exchanges tend to be rather formal (even tense and serious), they are generally scheduled (not spontaneous), and typically recurrent. We might round off the consideration of the scheduled recurrent type by giving an example of this kind of exchange.

Reporting to the boss

This example is from a very large telecommunications company in the Rhineland, where a senior production manager (five levels above the foreman) reports to his general manager boss. These are the points of the discussion:

1 The production manager reports on a contract the company has won in the face of international competition: it was in the morning newspaper but the boss had not seen it.

2 They discuss a production capacity problem at one of their factories in another town, and whom they are going to approach to sort it out.

3 They consider the background and achievements of a junior colleague, especially his breadth of experience in another company before he joined them. They decide to promote him and put him in charge of a special project. (In fact this younger manager is promoted later the same day; his project is to organise the production of a sophisticated component which has been designed and is at the prototype stage).

4 They discuss a project at another local manufacturing site under their control: it is going badly and they wonder if the situation can be improved by bringing in new blood.

5 They exchange views on a colleague working in development who would like to move to a post in production, and whether he is suitable.

6 They decide who should be responsible for maintaining and repairing testing equipment, and how the sections which develop this test equipment can be brought under the control of production.

7 The company has some workshops which make prototypes for the development sections; these workshops obviously serve development on a

one-to-one basis, but the general manager is keen that production should take overall control of them.

8 They evaluate the production engineering department: what this department is good at from the standpoint of production is method improvement and the development of inspection techniques, but they are not so good at evolving *cheaper* manufacturing methods.

9 Finally they turn to the question of component standardisation, which leads to a more general discussion of the interface between production and development; the production manager is directed to produce a working paper on how to achieve better co-operation between these two functions.

The above exchange is not only of substantive interest but brings out a number of general points as well. The higher the rank in management the more outward-looking are the typical concerns, is a precept illustrated by this exchange. These two managers are concerned with export orders, operations and problems in other company plants, some of them on distant locations. The analogous point is that they are not just concerned with the performance of their own subordinates in isolation but with the relationships between production and other corporate entities – the prototype workshops, development, production engineering. In short they are concerned with what the theorists call boundary management, with controlling and bettering these interfaces between production and contingent functions.

The last point in the exchange, 9, concerning component standardisation is worth a little elaboration. We are so used to treating as a joke Henry Ford's quip 'you can have any colour you like so long as it is black' that maybe we do not see why he said it. The basic point is that the organisation of production is immeasurably assisted by uniformity. Henry Ford inclines us to think of uniformity of the finished product (all black motor cars) but even more important is uniformity in component parts. If there are five models, but they are all assembled from the same twelve components in different numbers and combinations, this is a great advance on five models with separate component sets – but a difficult state of affairs to achieve. It is difficult to achieve because designers and development engineers do not think (primarily) in these terms. They think of the end result, of technical excellence, and they prescribe components in this vein, their choice also conditioned on occasion by habit and prejudice. They are not constantly asking themselves: can this new model be made with (some) components already used for other products. Yet to the extent to which such product standardisation is achieved there are gains in making purchasing, materials control and assembly more straightforward. A working paper on the relationship between development and production as requested by the general manager in the last example is a contribution to this desirable objective.

On another occasion the present writer recalls a Swedish managing director generalising about his job, saying that it consisted essentially of two things, of analysing a situation to produce plans which would lead to the desired state of affairs, and then choosing people capable of carrying them out. Put another way, the higher the rank in management, the more the individual is concerned with a certain kind of 'people work': with picking people, judging them, deciding whom to advance and how to match managers to assignments. The point comes out very well in the exchange between these two German managers at the telecommunications company. We have a special project – promote someone good to handle it; a project at another works is going badly – can we solve this problem with 'new blood'; a manager in development wants to join us in production – does he have the right qualities, and so on. An ancillary point is that there is an element of pure empire building in this managerial exchange (though oddly there is no phrase in German for 'empire building'). And there is also an empirical generalisation to be extracted from the dialogue, namely that the smaller the group (two is small!) the more explicit the organisational politics statements become – from the example of the meeting just discussed, how can we get a grip of the prototype workshops, or the sections which repair test equipment; how can we redefine (working paper first step) the relationship between development and production – in our favour.

So far we have considered scheduled recurrent meetings as a component of the work of most general and production managers, both by enumerating examples and by examining some in detail and offering an interpretative commentary. Let us look next at the second category of convened special purpose meetings, almost as important for British managers, and constituting an even larger proportion of the working time for German managers (see the tables in Chapter 1). The variety of purpose is much greater with these special purpose meetings, and there does not seem to be any simple summarising typology like that of production meetings, departmental meetings, and worker representative committees which we advanced for the range of scheduled recurrent meetings. A few examples will make this difference clear.

Special purpose meetings

First a senior project leader at the R & D establishment of a major British telecommunications company. In the course of two days this manager attended just one special purpose meeting: together with the other project leaders he went to a seminar conducted by the establishment's personnel officer on selection techniques and interviewing skills. This was highly relevant to the work of the establishment which was expanding rapidly with a consequent need to seek and appoint young graduate research staff in significant numbers.

The general manager in charge of a heavy fabrications unit whose departmental meeting was discussed earlier in this chapter was involved in four such special purpose meetings in two days of the study. First is a meeting with the export manager of his own company and the president of an American subsidiary doing subcontract work for them. The purpose is partly one of familiarisation on both sides, but with the undercurrent of advice from the general manager to the younger American president on how to optimise his operations. Second is a meeting with his works super-intendent and materials controller concerning a major order which is running late. The trio decide that the situation can be retrieved by night-shift working, carefully selecting high output workers for this night-shift, and overtime working to bridge the gap between the end of the normal working day and the commencement of the night-shift.

This company was expanding its business and like the R & D establish-ment in the last example had a need for new workers, in this case welders not electronics graduates. This is the subject of the third special purpose meeting, a discussion between the general manager and his production superintendent where they sift a set of applications, and decide whom to interview. Most of the applicants are from another part of the country and some are unemployed. This makes the selection of interviewees more difficult by bringing in questions about readiness to move, adaptability and motives, as well as trade competence. This meeting ended with the general manager calling a friend in a factory in the north and arranging to use his works as a base for interviewing and his workshop for practical skill tests for the applicants.

The last of the four meetings concerns industrial relations. The com-pany had just made its annual wage rise offer to the representatives of the various unions, and the unions had all rejected the offer as inadequate. The general manager and his production superintendent held a meeting with the senior convenor with the dual purpose of smoothing things over for the time being and averting any wildcat strike to put pressure on the company to raise the offer, and finding out what the unions would in fact settle for. People who have not been engaged in wage negotiations might not appreciate that there is often an element of poker playing. It usually helps to get the other side to show their hand before you show yours.

The next example also involves pay and productivity bargaining. The manager concerned is a packaging manager in a British food processing company, one level above that of the foreman. His company concluded a pay deal with its employees conditional on the development of a productivity package. This manager went to three special purpose meetings in a two-day period all relating to the productivity deal. The first is as part of a management team negotiating the terms of the productivity deal with representatives of the union. The second is a meeting called by the manager's boss and attended by other same-rank colleagues at which the boss propounds to his subordinate managers the gains to the company of the productivity deal just concluded, and answers questions on it. The third meeting is between the manager and his foremen in which he communicates the terms of the deal and explains how the foremen will be involved in its implementation.

Let us turn next to a much more senior manager, a manufacturing director of another British food processing company in charge of a works employing over 1,200 people. The head office is 200 miles away, so this manufacturing director is practically an on-site chief executive for the works with managers responsible for production, purchasing, personnel, warehouse and transport, project engineering and maintenance all reporting to him. His series of special purpose meetings are in a certain sense typical of those held by a top manager: they tend to be two-man meetings between the manager and various principal subordinates he has summoned, and to take place in his own office. In two days this manufacturing manager has eight such special purpose meetings:

1 With the production and maintenance managers to discuss a major plant repair.

2 A meeting with the head office auditor who has come to spend several days in the works. The manufacturing director suggests various particular things the auditor might like to investigate, including pallet labelling, a system for random checks on outgoing lorries, control of packaging materials, monitoring basic raw material usage and so on. This discussion is a timely reminder that the work of an auditor in industry is not limited to checking balances in ledgers.

3 The manufacturing director summons the project engineering manager

to discuss the programme, and to consider possible expenditure reductions.

4 He discusses with his personnel manager the replacement of a colleague forced to retire because of ill-health – it is a sensitive appointment.

5 The manufacturing director receives a general state-of-the-plant report from his production manager, before the latter leaves for a weekend course.

6 In a meeting with the purchasing manager they consider their general supply strategy.

7 A second meeting with the personnel manager covers a discussion of a forward-looking personnel plan stating the company's presumptive manpower needs.

8 A discussion with the project engineering director and the transport manager to devise a budgetary rationale for updating part of the transport fleet.

This set of discussions instituted by a senior manager are another good illustration of priorities and preoccupations at the top. Again several of these discussions are forward-looking – the personnel plan, a major repair which will take months to set up and execute, the supplies question. This last, supplies, is a nice blend of strategy and politics. The company uses coal as a raw material, it has to be high quality coal, and so far this has only been available in the UK. The purchasing manager has now located an equally good quality source in South Africa, and it is cheaper. But there are political and logistical considerations. Should they switch to this South African source, save money and maintain quality? They discuss it and decide against. There is a second supplies question. They use oil, the prices of the oil company which supplies them have become uncompetitive and there are cheaper alternatives. Yet this oil company has proved reliable and kept up supplies even in times of international shortage. Should they change suppliers? They hit on a way to run two suppliers and keep both happy.

So we have in the case of this manufacturing director a forward-looking orientation which has emerged in looking at the work of some other senior managers. There is also a strong money orientation. The higher up a manager is the more poignant is concern with the company's financial objectives. It comes out in this case in the form of briefing the auditor, instituting expenditure reductions on engineering projects, analysing the budgetary implications of equipment (transport) renewal, and so on.

In this set of meetings we see again the concern with picking people, which is characteristic of senior management posts. The colleague to be replaced, 4 above, is senior, it is a sensitive appointment, and there is no single and obvious heir apparent. There is a more general consideration, which is that in meetings with immediate subordinates a top manager is bound to be assessing their quality and potential in an on-going way. He never knows when he may be asked to pick a deputy, or a successor, or respond to a head office request to find someone for a special mission.

Finally in connection with this manufacturing director we find a timely reminder that management work, at however senior a level, is also concerned with current operations and some small-scale things. In this particular case the discussion with the production manager, 5 above, included reducing the number of portacabins (rented) at the works, and getting employees to clean up some work areas.

So far we have illustrated the range and substance of these special purpose meetings by giving examples from four companies in Britain. Now the difference is not a black and white one but these same special purpose meetings in Germany do have a flavour of their own in the sense of there being some recurrent themes. We will conclude the discussion of special purpose meetings by taking three examples from German companies making respectively medical equipment, bulldozers and flexible metal tubes.

Special purpose meetings German style

Our first example is a quite senior production manager who reports to the board of directors in a medical equipment factory. During the two days of the study this manager holds no scheduled recurrent meetings (his only one is a monthly departmental meeting chaired by himself) but there are two special purpose meetings. The first with his safety officer, maintenance engineer, manager responsible for building extensions and his personal assistant is concerned with how to implement new legislation in Germany for the protection of the environment. The key issue is the discharge of fluid waste and its treatment, and the problem the company faces is that they do not know how much water they discharge, if it is polluted and if so how badly. So the meeting sets up a monitoring and analysis exercise to find the answers to these preliminary questions so that they can decide what the company must do to conform to the new law. The discussion is peppered with denunciations of civil servants who are held to have been unhelpful to industry by their confused specification of what is required under the new legislation. German managers have a tendency to vent on civil servants the scorn and irritation which in Britain is reserved for politicians.

This manager's second special purpose meeting is with all his subordinate production managers, their engineering advisers, and the purchasing manager, and it is a machinery purchase meeting. The decision to buy a number of (vastly expensive) machines has already been taken: the purpose of this meeting is to decide which ones to buy from what supplier. A twist to this discussion is that they decide to place an important order for new machines with a British manufacturer. That morning newspapers in West Germany announced a fall in the value of the pound sterling against the Deutschmark. One of the managers at this meeting suggests that at this 'dream price' they should buy more machines than they need from England and stockpile them. They do not actually decide to do this, but the suggestion is taken quite seriously.

The second German example is a works director at a bulldozer factory. His only meeting of this kind is to receive a group of visiting Swedes who are considering buying an enormous bulldozer for their civil engineering firm. The party is made up of the owner of the civil engineering firm, his manufacturing manager and a representative of their bank who will finance the purchase. The German works director received the party, sales-talked them (in English), demonstrated the bulldozer, discussed technical specifications with the Swedish manufacturing manager, gave them a personal tour of the works and took them out to dinner.

The third German example is a general manager in charge of a division of his company with sales and R & D reporting to him as well as production and production-related departments. The meeting is with a selection of colleagues from production, R & D, sales and their patents section. The problem the meeting faces is this. The division has been making one of its products in a light-weight alloy. There were no rival manufacturers (anywhere) and it had been a success. More recently another German company had begun to make the same product in the same alloy and its design was regarded as superior (the rival product was on display at the meeting and attracted much admiring attention). The interesting thing is that a number of options are simply not discussed at this meeting. There is no consideration of giving up this product line, dividing the market with the rival, or simply finding a loop-hole in the patent law and attacking the rival with his own product differentiated by a meaningless modification. The assumption is that the only possible riposte is to come up with an even better design which will recapture the market, and the discussion focused on the means and ways of design. At one stage the meeting veers off this point, but is recalled sharply by the chairman's directive: 'You are here to design a better product, not to find some crack in the patent law.'

It would be possible to offer more examples in the same vein but the difference in emphasis is already clear. General and senior production managers in Germany have a tendency to see their work in more technical terms. They are more concerned with what they call *Technik* than with the Anglo-Saxon notion of 'management' as something more general. This difference comes out even in the above exemplary list of special purpose meetings: the technical implications of new legislation, machinery purchase (money no object), design work, defining sales as a technical operation, the presumptive capacity to produce an even better product as the company's strongest weapon, and so on.

It is important to be alive to this difference for two reasons. The first is practical. Anyone who deals with West Germany should know that his or her counterparts are probably operating on a more technical and specialist model, and are product-centred rather than profit-centred. The second reason is that it is the international, and thus homogeneous, aspects of management which are typically emphasised in management writing and in the media. Against this background it does no harm to show that there are some differences of style and emphasis in management from country to country, and our vehicle for doing so just happens to be the Anglo-German comparison.

Ad hoc discussions

The third type of exchange defined in the previous chapter is *ad hoc* discussions, typically brief, two-man, unscheduled, one-off communication episodes. By definition, they are more numerous, more varied and more fragmented than the formal meetings already discussed. The *ad hoc* discussion is more particularly the prerogative of the junior manager, or the manager in a small company, and such *ad hoc* discussions represent a higher proportion of working time for German managers than for their English colleagues. We will give one example to show at least some of the issues which may be dealt with in this way without benefit of a more formal meeting.

The example chosen is prototypical in one way since the manager concerned is a middle manager in a smallish (750 employees) family firm in north Germany. On the other hand, it is unusual because of the prevailing weather conditions! During the two-day period of the study a blizzard was raging. By the end of the first day numerous local authority districts outside the town where the works is situated had declared states of emergency, the town was completely cut off by road and connected to the outside world only by a railway line to Hamburg, and the town administration imposed a 100 DM spot fine for anyone attempting to leave by car on the grounds that they would become a charge on the rescue services. The twenty or so *ad hoc* discussions in which this manager is involved are a curious mix of 'business as usual' and at the same time a reflection of the weather problems:

1 With the safety engineer on (a) safety matters, and (b) rulings of the works doctor on individual employee cases, i.e. whether the health problems of these workers have implications for industrial safety.

2 With a foreman on (a) provision of internal transport, and (b) permission to institute overtime working.

3 With one of the superintendents on the current investment plan (machinery and equipment purchase).

4 A quick briefing session with the production director (the manager's boss).

5 Discussing intended changes in the factory layout with one of the superintendents.

6 Advising a senior foreman on the first afternoon that workers may be sent home because of the bad weather; this was followed by a tour of the factory with the manager giving the same message to all his foremen. One asked what would happen on the following day and received the reply 'We will work tomorrow' (they more or less did; most of the workers lived in the town and were not affected by the driving restriction, but many of the managers in outlying villages were).

7 Discussing implications of the weather conditions with the personnel manager.

8 Talking to the maintenance manager about various preventive and remedial manoeuvres (hiring snow ploughs, salting and sanding factory roads, instituting snow clearing teams to start at 5 a.m., etc.). The best bit was the maintenance manager telling his boss with the manner of one imparting impending doom that without further supplies they would run out of central heating fuel in May: it was 14 February.

9 With one of the superintendents on the problem of missing personnel.

10 Exchanging weather-crisis information with the personnel manager.

11 Discussing a defective transformer with a superintendent; it has been put out of action by melting snow dripping down a ventilation shaft. They respond by turning off the lights to save power (but running most of the machines) until the transformer is repaired.

12 Advising two foremen what to do with their men during the power cut (machine maintenance and snow clearing).

13 Urging the electrical design engineer to repair the transformer.

14 Explaining causes of transformer failure to the safety officer.

15 Lobbying the managing director for a new roof to be included in the current investment plan (citing the transformer incident as divine judgment on failure to modernise buildings).

16 Briefing the managing director's PA on emergency arrangements.

17 Discussions with various foremen about the arrangements for the late shift on the second day; arranging transport for workers, offering to pay taxi fares.

18 Giving instructions to clerks with nothing to do to snow clear car parks.

Even from this one example certain things are clear about the function of *ad hoc* discussions. They are fragmented, wide ranging, and serve a variety of small objectives. They are a standard means for passing on bits of information. These discussions are often triggered off by crisis or emergency; many of them, and not only in the example quoted above, are in the form of attempts to put right things that have gone wrong. There is also an in-built tendency to 'clustering' with *ad hoc* discussions, in the sense that one incident will set off a series, as with the transformer breakdown example we have just considered. Lastly, though it does not arise in the above example, *ad hoc* discussions are also precipitated by personal antipathies and disagreements. These disagreements have to be (largely) avoided in more formal meetings with others present, so the *ad hoc* discussion is a way of doing business on the side where it is necessary to by-pass difficulties between individuals.

Touring the works

As we showed in the last chapter, general and production managers in both countries spend getting on for one-fifth of their working time on the shop floor or touring the works. While there are one or two examples of managers in both countries (especially Britain) who do not do it at all, the majority certainly do, and traditional management wisdom is in favour of it. There are some justifications for this activity which, if they are not exactly intangible, cannot be counted or quantified. Spending time in the works for managers is a matter of showing one's face, being seen, keeping one's finger on the pulse (English) or not becoming *betriebsblind* (German – blind to the reality of the company), spreading good will, and making oneself available. But these tours of the works are also a vast multifarious checking exercise, especially for managers with a direct stake in production.

First, these tours are an opportunity to check the quality of raw materials, bought-out-parts, components, finished goods coming off the machines or in inspection, the quality of fabrication or assembly work, and to monitor the production process in process plants, even to check the checks that the quality control section are (should be) making.

Second, time spent in the works is also about checking the plant and machinery. Production managers look and see how machines are functioning, and ask operators about it; they check whether new machines have been delivered, or installed, or brought into production and are running well; they check whether repairs are necessary, or whether repairs instituted are progressing well and perhaps already complete; they can check on the progress of any building or decorating work that is going on and talk to sub-contractors, outside repairmen and installation crews; at the same time the tour is a chance to look at the ancillary buildings – the rest room, locker rooms, boiler house, generating plant, packing sheds, warehouse, telex room and even the car parks.

Third, and moving now to the social and political dimension, these tours are a chance to have 'a quick word' with people, as we have emphasised in the earlier discussion of the continuum of meetings. This encompasses greetings, polite enquiries, occasional reprimands, exhortations about costs, rates, methods and deadlines; explaining contingencies and new procedures; sometimes passing on information systematically (as in the case of the German manager in the blizzard-torn factory).

Fourth, and it is a more specific version of the previous point, time spent in the works facilitates a trouble-shooting role where the manager not only identifies some problem but engages in action to solve it. Three particular themes here are:

1 Intervention to speed up jobs, for instance re-routing them, making swop-overs between conventional and numerically controlled machines, and re-assigning on the spot priorities.

2 Quality trouble-shooting, especially in Germany. Noting that there is something wrong with the product or process and trying to figure out where it starts and why it is happening. This involves things like checking inputs, watching repeated machine operations, asking operators, devising little tests, studying operations at a crucial point on, say, an assembly line, sometimes phoning around to get a more informed opinion.

3 Industrial relations trouble-shooting, especially in Britain. This covers things like being available to receive complaints, observing directly the context of some industrial relations incident, collecting circumstantial evidence or even impressions, asking for second opinions without making

too much of a thing of it, trying to defuse incidents at an early stage and looking for signs of problems that have not even happened.

Lastly the tour is a kind of visual management by exception exercise. Apart from considerations of quality and technical function the manager going around the works has an eye cocked for anything that should not be there or is out of place.

It is important to talk about the detail of what managers may achieve in the time they spend on the shop floor because it is too easy to dismiss this as just 'strolling around'. The tour is management work.

Telephoning as management work

The managers in our study made some 1,282 telephone calls, and as a proportion of working time activity it approaches the 10 per cent mark. But trying to classify the content or context of such telephoning is awesomely difficult. There are, however, some general comments which may be helpful.

It is possible to divide the calls roughly into information calls and action initiative calls, though the demarcation is not always clear-cut. The former type, that is, request or provide information (what time are they coming?, can I have a breakdown on . . .?, this is what's been happening while you've been away, and so on), while the latter type tend to make something happen (come over straight away and we'll talk about it, have it installed this afternoon, promote him straight away, set up the tests for Tuesday, etc.).

Then one can distinguish between internal and external calls, and the majority for all ranks of managers in the study are internal calls, though the proportion of external calls goes up with rank. For those concerned with the organisation of production external telephone calls are typically to suppliers, usually complaining about delay.

There is a similar distinction between incoming calls (received by the manager in question) and outgoing calls (initiated by the manager). In both countries the majority of calls are outgoing, which supports our conception of the manager as man of action, controlling his own destiny, pursuing his own war aims. Having said this, there is a difference of degree between the proportions for the two groups of managers. In the case of the British managers 50 per cent of all telephone calls are outgoing, but the corresponding figure for the Germans is over 71 per cent. The reason for the difference is not an easy thing to be sure about, but it is noticeable that there is a disaster element in the English case. Quite a few incoming calls, that is, report some problem, and especially industrial relations problems (see the next chapter).

It seems to us that there is also a German quirk in the managerial use of telephones. It serves the ends, that is, of 'group recrimination'. When something happens which a German manager does not like, in the sense of some other person or department having let him down or frustrated his efforts, there is a tendency to denounce the offending party in a series of subsequent telephone conversations. There is an interesting twist to this: it is not usually done in the sense of establishing an alibi – 'I would have had it done on time but now the purchasing department have let us down . . . .' Rather it is done with a flourish or moral indignation as though the listener will understandably relish this opportunity to condemn evil. A final point about telephoning as a management activity is that its incidence varies enormously from manager to manager. In the case of one German manager telephoning took up 20 per cent of his entire working time, while one of the English managers at the other extreme made no telephone calls at all. We would like to suggest at the end of the chapter that there is a personal style element in all this.

Desk work

In both countries managers spend around 12 per cent of their time working alone in their own offices. This opens up the question, what exactly are they doing? Put in management textbook terms it is time spent planning and controlling, or contributing to the exercise of control by others by providing them with information. But it is possible to break this down into something more tangible.

To start with, most managers spend a little of this time controlling their own work and objectives. They make lists of what they want to do in a day, or the following day, prioritise them, tick off things done, write little outcome notes, reminders, and aide-mémoires. In a similar vein they occasionally prepare agendas for meetings, or more often prepare for meetings by looking through relevant documents, making notes for their own benefit on points they want to raise, or just psyching themselves up to argue a case before colleagues and perhaps superiors.

Then the desk work heading covers report writing, though this is not a major activity. Although the need to write reports, at least substantial reports, goes up with rank, so does the tendency to do it at home. Conversely, there is a certain amount of report reading, with the Germans in particular showing a penchant for technical reports.

Next there is everything to do with correspondence: reading letters, memos and telexes; dictating letters and memos to a secretary or more often on to a dictating machine (there are occasional hand-drafted letters); and then checking and signing outgoing correspondence originated by the managers themselves and sometimes by their subordinates. It should perhaps be added that managers do not get much mail in the conventional sense of letters, nor do they send many letters. Neither is mail given any kind of priority treatment; this is especially true with the Germans who tend to read the incoming mail after lunch in the belief that anything requiring fast action would have come by telex.

The major desk work activity, however, is reading, checking and monitoring a lot of internal correspondence mostly in the form of works documents and computer print-outs. For production managers the most common are analysis of costs, job-rates, shop-loading, production schedules, breakdowns of the output of particular sections, analysis of the wage bill, calculations of the cost of scrap, rejects, and reworking of jobs, sales forecasts, breakdowns of job orders, and sometimes sales quotations, especially where the production manager has to approve the cost of some modification or extra.

Managers tend to complain about the volume of works documents, and indeed the main function of some of the computer print-outs is to protect the desk top from spilled coffee. On the other hand, at least some of these documents, especially those dealing with costs and schedules, are important control instruments and diagnostic tools for managers. On many of these documents managers do a kind of management by exception job, scanning them quickly to look for (nasty) surprises and anomalies – why did we make so much money in March, why was the overtime bill so high last week, why is there a bottleneck in the welding section, why are my unit's telephone costs higher than anyone else's?

Pattern and choice

So far we have presented a typology of management activity, shown how a sample of managers from two countries actually spend their time in terms of this typology, illustrated all the types of work activity in some detail, and provided an interpretative commentary. On occasion we have also drawn attention to the fact that there are lots of differences between the individual managers in terms of the distribution of time between these activities (in telephoning, for example). To take this last point a little further, one of the German managers spent over 40 per cent of his time in tours of the works while another of the Germans and several of the British spent no time at all in this way. Or again, some of the managers spent no time on scheduled recurrent meetings, and a smaller number had neither scheduled recurrent meetings nor special purpose meetings, only *ad hoc* discussions.

In trying to explain both the general results for the group as a whole, as well as the individual differences within the group, the danger is probably that one is too rational. There is a tendency to think that it must all be patterned in some way, one just has to find the right key — perhaps it is size of company, or branch of industry, or type of production technology, or whatever. In fact we found very few systematic connections on the basis of our sample of thirty-six companies and forty-one managers closely observed. Indeed it is difficult to get beyond the following (not very exciting) generalisations:

1 The most senior general managers have the highest proportion of time spent on desk work.

2 The higher ranking managers in the larger firms tend to spend a higher proportion of their time in formal meetings (types 1a and 1b).

3 The converse point: the few superintendents (with foremen as their immediate subordinates) spent a proportion of time on the shop floor which is higher than the sample average (but not the highest).

In other words there are substantial differences between the managers under the several activity headings which do not seem to be explained in any rationally patterned way. So perhaps a different explanation is in order, namely that these types of management activity represent a set of alternatives. In this connection consider the following propositions:

1 Frequent general purpose meetings (1a) reduce the need for special purpose meetings (1b).

2 Frequent informal exchanges (1c, *ad hoc* discussions) reduce the need for both kinds of formal meeting (1a and 1b).

3 Extensive tours of the works offer ample scope for having brief exchanges thereby reducing the need for even 1c-type *ad hoc* discussions.

4 Frequent communication by telephone may be an alternative to formal meetings (1a and 1b), and even to *ad hoc* discussions (1c).

5 Telephoning as a means of communication and control may even reduce the need for tours of the works.

In other words we are suggesting that there is variety in the ways in which the work, or work objectives, are accomplished. This variety is reflected in the varying proportions of time allocated to the different types of activity in our scheme. This may seem a modest contention but it should be said that it is not comprehended by the existing literature which tends to explain such variations impersonally. Furthermore, our finding, that managers to some extent choose between sets of activities to accomplish their designs, also gives a tangible meaning to the vague notion of management style.

Summary

This second chapter has built on the typology of management work presented in Chapter 1 by offering examples of the various kinds of formal meeting, and in some cases detailing the issues dealt with at such meetings. We argued that there are three main kinds of scheduled recurrent meeting – production meetings, departmental meetings and worker representative meetings. No such simple categories can be adduced to cover the range of convened special purpose meetings, and examples of these special purpose meetings were also given. In the discussion and exemplification of these formal meetings we pursued two other aims: pointing to differences between senior and junior managers, and noting things that distinguish British from German managers.

From this discussion of the various kinds of meeting we moved to discuss and illustrate other elements of management work in the form of informal discussions, telephoning, tours of the works and desk/office work. We showed that the proportion of time devoted to these activities varies markedly from individual to individual, and these variations do not appear to be explicable in terms of some obvious factor such as rank, company size or nationality. In response to this unexplained variety we suggest that managers are in fact choosing between different ways of achieving their objectives, that the different proportions of time spent on these activities are a manifestation of personal style.

Further reading

SUNE CARLSON, *Executive Behaviour*, Strombergs, Stockholm, 1951. This is the first and most famous study of the way a group of Swedish chief executives spend their time and is well worth reading. It is difficult to get hold of but the British Lending Library (Boston Spa) have a copy.
ROSEMARY STEWART, *Managers and their Jobs*, Pan, 1967. It is an excellent British study of the work of a mixed sample of 160 managers.
HENRY MINTZBERG, *The Nature of Managerial Work*, Harper & Row, New York, 1973. This is the best available American study which uses data

about management work to formulate the idea of some basic and alternative management roles.

There is a more detailed analysis of the work of samples of British and German managers in two reports by the present writer:

S.P. HUTTON and P.A. LAWRENCE, 'The Work of Production Managers: Case Studies of Manufacturing Companies in West Germany', report to the Department of Industry, 1979.

S.P. HUTTON and P.A. LAWRENCE, 'The Work of Production Managers: Case Studies of Manufacturing Companies in the United Kingdom', report to the Science and Engineering Research Council, 1982.

Both are obtainable from the University of Loughborough library.

Discussion questions

1   How adequate is the typology of management work propounded in Chapter 1? Suggest an alternative.
2   What does it mean to say that management is about communications?
3   What differences do you see so far between managers in Britain and in Germany? Is the existence of such differences significant?
4   Is it reasonable for senior production managers and general managers to spend so much time in tours of the works? Would not this time be better spent in strategic planning?
5   Is the office work which managers do, as described in Chapter 2, the work which they *ought* to do?
6   Try to develop a profile of a senior or general manager in terms of responsibilities, preoccupations and work patterns.

3

Relations between departments

Right at the start of this book we argued that one reason for a focus on production managers is that production is such a central function. This chapter will not take an exclusively production-oriented view of the relationships between the various management functions or departments, but production is a very helpful starting point.

Central and indispensable

Production is not just a central function, but the most central function. In the same way that West Germany has borders with more other countries than any other state in Europe, the production function in industry has contacts and dealings with more other departments, this being one of the points which was illustrated with the aid of some organisation charts in the first chapter. In fact, contacts and dealings are words which are not sufficiently strong since production is locked in dependence on so many of these other departments and sections. Production depends on sales for orders, for work to actually do; it may depend on R & D or design for products or models to manufacture; it depends on production engineering to devise manufacturing methods and to sort out technical problems; on purchasing to obtain materials and components; on production planning and control to set up production schedules and oversee them; on quality control to define standards and pass completed jobs; and perhaps on a transport or distribution section to 'ship out' finished work.

Production is not only central, but indispensable to a company's operations. Again, as we showed in the first chapter, probably the majority of companies are without R & D, and many do not have a design department. Smaller companies do not have a personnel section, and there are even companies which do not have any sales function, where for instance, all their output is taken by one large purchaser-customer, or where all the produce is destined for some other part of the group. But all companies have production.

Functions and status

So far by way of introduction we have suggested that companies have a number of functions and departments, but these vary in the extent and intensity of their relations with each other. It is perhaps not obvious to people whose work does not bring them into contact with industry but these various functions also tend to be differentiated by status, though here we speak with particular reference to Britain. Finance is a high status function: it is nice and clean, it is about money, and tends to be staffed by a well-trained personnel most of whom have accountancy qualifications generally regarded as degree equivalent. Being in finance is also to be drawn into the company's decision making: finance is about measuring profitability, allocating funds, raising money, predicting performance and budgetary control. These are all activity-decision areas which affect others thereby heightening the esteem of finance, and furthermore these exercises are not readily comprehensible to the layman, and indeed are surrounded by some mystique. Sales and/or marketing is another high prestige function. Again it is clean, in the sense of being far removed from the shop floor and dealing with presumptively stroppy workers and nasty bits of metal – this cleanliness syndrome is important in the British scheme of things. One reflection of the fact that finance and sales are high status areas of management work is the fact that a disproportionate number of chief executives/managing directors have a sales or finance background.[1] Salary is another indicator, and again there is British data to suggest that managers is these two functions are paid above the executive average, holding rank and company size constant.[2]

At the other end of this prestige scale in British industry comes production and, it is often held, design. It is ironic that production does not rank higher in informal esteem, given its centrality, indispensability and responsibilities, but the fact has to be faced. The 'case against production' in this sense is an amalgam of physically poor working conditions by managerial standards (noise, swarf, solvents and all that), pressure to get things done on time, vulnerability to industrial relations problems and the endless dependencies on other functions already referred to. There are three important qualifications to make to this view that production is a low status function. First, production managers are very numerous, much more numerous than, say, finance managers, and so by sheer weight of numbers they make themselves felt and some of them get to the top. Second, a related point which was touched on in the first chapter, is the fact that many big companies are organised into geographically separate semi-independent works, and the headship of these is very much a mark of career success, typically achieved by moving through a series of line production management posts (an example is given in the discussion of Figure 1.3 in Chapter 1). Third, this idea that production is 'a cinderella function' gained currency in Britain in the 1970s, it attracted a lot of attention in the debate about Britain's comparatively poor economic performance, and stimulated a lot of research.[3] The upshot of all this has been to turn the tide in favour of production. Posts in production now are more highly regarded than ten years ago, and production appears to be attracting a bigger share of graduates and others with superior business school qualifications. There are also companies which are appointing graduates as foremen, even if not on a long-term basis.

The case of design is more difficult to explain, especially in view of the widely held and probably justifiable belief that inventiveness is a British strength. On the other hand Britain is not a country with a strong engineering tradition or strongly developed technical culture, as for example are Japan or West Germany,[4] and this tends to depress the status of design. The rather low standing of design is also probably connected with the rather high standing of finance: British business culture has a strong vein of profit now rather than technical excellence in ten years' time. The result has often been a failure to develop products from technical breakthroughs, and a willingness to go down-market in terms of product for the sake of calculable sales revenue in the short term, leaving the technically sophisticated ventures with their attendant risks to others. In this climate the designer is often seen as a bit of a nuisance rather than a corporate asset.

The fact remains that functions are not only differentiated by the work they do, their centrality and the nature of their interface (contact, relationship) with other departments, but also on a continuum of informal prestige ranging from sales and finance through personnel, R & D, purchasing, and other technical functions to design and production.

Sociology and sub-unit power play

There are two important linked ideas that have come out of the sociology of organisations. The first is that organisations, once created, have a tendency to become larger than life, to get bigger not smaller, to take on more objectives, acquire more resources, plan for their eternal existence and, above all, develop ideas to justify their goals and methods of achieving them. The American sociologist Philip Selznick in particular has elaborated these ideas. One of his books entitled *Leadership in Administration* argues that the key function of heads of organisations is to institutionalise the values that support the organisation's existence and objectives.[5] Institutionalise, that is, in the sense of sustain and propagate and personally represent. In another book Selznick describes the setting up of the Tennessee Valley Authority under the Roosevelt administration in 1933, an organisation charged with damming the Tennessee River in order to prevent flooding, provide irrigation and, above all, to generate hydroelectric power with the further aim of attracting electricity using industry to a relatively poor and backward area.[6] The TVA was an unusual organisation, neither state nor federal, nor private nor voluntary. In its early years the TVA leaders developed what was called 'the grass roots ideology', suggesting that the Authority took its power and purpose from the (local) people whose needs it served. In practice this was largely eyewash: TVA leaders did, and still do, pretty well what they want, but the grass roots ideology is a very handy weapon for keeping the federal and state authorities out of it, and allowing the TVA to go its own way. This then is the first point, that organisations tend to enhance their powers and be resourceful in justifying their activities and objectives.

The second and related idea is that formal organisations usually find it necessary to create sub-units (departments, sections, functions and so on) all contributing to the overall end but by different activities. Business firms are an obvious example where different sub-units are created to buy materials, organise production, sell the output and so on. These sub-units have, and are meant to have, a specialised competence, so that people in the finance department really do know more about, say, the analysis of profitability than anyone else in the company. It is a short step from this specialised competence, and a heightened consciousness of it, to an overvaluing of the contribution of the sub-unit to the whole organisation, where the output and performance of the sub-unit becomes an end in itself. In other words, organisations are founded, establish specialised sub-units with particular responsibilities, these get 'out of hand', and a certain amount of empire building, internal friction and hostile stereotyping within the company ensue.

There is a further paradox. Not only have companies not intended these developments, but they are not very good at handling them. The formal resource for dealing with rivalries and hostilities between departments is for higher management to exercise some co-ordinative control. This may be effective, but there are certainly limitations on its effectiveness. One is that higher management often simply does not know what to do for the best, and therefore does not know how to regulate and arbitrate. When the head of R & D claims they simply need another eighteen months and £2m for a breakthrough that will make the company handsome profits for twenty years, and finance say they have heard it all before and R & D have already wasted £12m, and the production director is lobbying for £2m to be spent on new machinery, and marketing are asking for a concerted sales drive in North America, and the purchasing director is claiming that if he had freedom to locate new suppliers it would be worth more to the company than a 20 per cent growth in market share, *and* all of them are attacking each other and manoeuvring for personal (departmental) advantage, what should the managing director do? Another problem is that managing directors do not spring fully armed into existence like warriors from dragons' teeth; they have their past, experience and hang-ups. Perhaps the managing director is an ex-marketing man who *knows* you cannot get anywhere without a share of the American market, and short-circuits the other arguments.

Two things follow from all this. The first is that friction and rivalries between functions are a very common part of the life of companies, not some extraordinary indication of inefficiency or waywardness. The second is that, since the official means for regulating these rivalries are usually inadequate, a lot of unofficial regulation and informal trading takes place. Consider the following, admittedly rather extreme, example from another American study.

Staff-line conflict

It is not fashionable any more but some years ago management theorists used to emphasise the distinction between staff and line managers. Line managers are ones with responsibility for plant, output and results. Production managers and general managers in charge of works and manufacturing units are examples *par excellence* of line managers. Staff are rather advisers, people employed by the company to use their specialist knowledge and training to advise and improve things such as manufacturing methods, information systems, training, the best use of the company's human resources, and so on.

The American sociologist Melville Dalton made a study of the relationship between staff and line in three companies in the USA. The relationship was a fairly tense one, marked by unflattering stereotypes on both sides, the line viewing the staff as impractical idealists, and the staff seeing the line as obstructionist power mongers. This clash of interest was made worse by socio-educational differences where the staff were younger, more highly educated, and with more trendy life styles, while the line were older, better paid and, above all, more powerful in the organisation.

In this situation the staff tended to become demoralised by the line's rejection of their bright ideas, and it seemed that the only way out in the middle term was to join the line (more pay and more power). The more enterprising staff advisers made deals with line managers not to make any problems for them *and* to transfer to these line managers part of their staff budget for experimental work. This would allow the line manager in question to save on his own operating budget and appear to run his section with commendable economy. This would put up the stock of the line manager, who in turn would use his influence to get the staff man promoted to a line post when a vacancy arose. This is a strong example, bordering on corruption. Much informal manoeuvring is based on nothing more than doing people favours, thereby building up influence and a constituency of colleagues and contacts who will be willing to 'help you out'. Consider a British example.

Coping with a transport strike

In the winter of 1979 there was a lorry drivers' strike in Britain, one that became famous for secondary picketing. This means that the striking drivers picketed not only their own employers, but also the premises of customers awaiting deliveries. Not long after this strike the present writer had the chance to ask the general manager of a works in southern England how he had coped with this strike. The manager had taken three moves to maintain his supplies of raw materials and components as well as 'shipping out' finished goods.

1 He had hired some lorries and drivers from a French transport firm (the works are close to the Channel ports).

2 He had managed to get control of a number of lorries usually assigned to other works in the group.

3 He had contacted many of his firm's suppliers and urged them to make an exception of his works and maintain deliveries.

As a result of these measures this manager claimed that the strike had made little impact on his operations, but the three measures are different in kind. The first is purely a matter of hard-headed initiative. Anyone could do it if they have the will and the nerve. The second is much more a reflection of this manager's personal standing in the group; not everyone would try (or still less be allowed) to sequestrate the transport of other works. But it is the third which is most interesting.

This manager has always made a practice of treating drivers from other firms (mainly suppliers) well. Drivers would be sent off to the canteen for a free meal, or given a rest while local employees unloaded the truck; the manager would look after them if they needed over-night accommodation, would have his workers mend their punctures or his electricians fix faults on the vehicles. All this enabled him to tell suppliers in an emergency that their drivers would make an exception and cross picket lines for his works.

So far the argument has been in general terms. Departments are distinguished by activity, purpose and centrality, and sometimes by status differences and even socio-cultural considerations as well. Thus, although they are 'all working for the same company', it is not surprising that friction and rivalries develop. Organisational sociologists have explored and on occasion documented the fact that these departments (sub-units with specialised competence) come to view their contribution as over-important and an end in itself (empire building and doing down rivals). Since the official means for regulating such rivalries are imperfect, much of the regulation is informal, in terms of wheeling and dealing and the exploitation of personal influence. In such a situation the most powerful resource is having a lot of people willing to help you out because of past favours or indulgence. Let us turn next to one or two classic cases of such rivalry in industry.

Production versus sales

There is a famous study by Keith Lockyer of the Bradford Management Centre in which samples of managers from finance, marketing, personnel and production are asked, among other things, to classify their relation with a range of other functions as satisfactory or unsatisfactory. The result is an instructive 'who hates whom' in British industry table, included in an article in *Management Today* describing the findings of the survey.[7]

It emerges from this table that managers from finance and personnel are well-adjusted, tolerant characters with a few grievances against colleagues in other departments. The marketing managers are less happy with the state of the world, and sizeable proportions of them describe the relationship with R & D, and of course production, as unsatisfactory. But it is the production managers themselves who really go to town: substantial proportions of them categorise the relationship with every other function as unsatisfactory, with marketing/sales coming in for considerable criticism.

What is the nature of this conflict between sales and production? It is important to grasp that it is not local or personal. It is in the logic of the situation. Consider the differences of interest and emphasis:

1 Sales like to be able to offer a wide range of products since it opens up a wider potential market: production like to restrict the product range for ease of manufacture.

2 Production have a more pervasive interest in standardisation and uniformity; this makes it easier to organise supply, sub-contracting and manufacture: sales have no particular interest in this, and sometimes do not understand the implications of variety.

3 Sales like to be able to offer customers modifications to standard products, which may help them to clinch a deal: production know that modifications mean hassle.

4 Sales like new models and product changes; it gives them a chance to offer potential customers something 'really new': production know that model changes mean tooling up, imponderables (how are we going to make something we have never made before?) and teething troubles.

5 Sales like short lead times (the lead time is the time it takes to produce something from when the order is accepted); it means they can tempt potential customers by offering them the goods 'yesterday': production like long lead times knowing from bitter experience all the things that can go wrong and slow them up.

6 Sales like to be able to under-cut stated lead times ('usually it takes six weeks, but if you give us the order today we will deliver in four'): production fear their inability to meet such tight deadlines.

7 Sales often have a general philosophy of get the order first and worry about how to fill it afterwards (especially in a recession): production tend to err on the side of caution.

8 The two also have a different orientation to price. Sales usually favour lower prices to make the product more competitive (and their job easier); production also want the product to be competitive but fear the consequences of price reductions which may make it difficult for them to keep within manufacturing budgets.

The above list is something of an ideal type. Not all these issues are controversial all the time, but some of them are in most companies most of the time. The result is that representatives of sales and production do fight about prices and lead times, modifications and 'specials', the wisdom of model changes and programmes for standardisation. It is made more complicated by the fact that many companies do not manufacture to order, in the sense of beginning work on something for a known customer; they manufacture against sales forecasts, calculations of salesmen as to how many of what they hope to be able to sell in the future. These forecasts are sometimes wrong, and there is no sure formula for getting them right.

There is a final imponderable in all this. Many of the choices listed above, between say short and long lead times, standard products or modified products, involve trade-offs. To put it simply, the company can offer the customer anything he wants, but it will cost more. So the customer should in theory be asked to pay more, but the company may fear it will lose business by asking for more. There is not any satisfactory answer to this. The company does not usually know how its sales fortunes will be affected by changes in the mix of price, quality, choice, speed of delivery and so on. Even given these imponderables, however, it is surprising how often companies do not formulate a policy on such issues and stick to it in the middle term: a common policy is simply 'muddling through'.

Design and production

The relationship between design and production is not usually so explicitly antipathetic as that between production and sales, yet there are similar contradictions of viewpoint and orientation. Indeed one might describe this relationship as one of serialised misapprehension. To start with, design are oriented to technical excellence, whereas production are oriented to feasibility. The two functions have different time perspectives. Production managers tend to think in terms of production cycle time, or the lead time for dominant products, or about accounting periods and how much they will have made by the end of the next quarter or whatever. Design, of course, tend to have a longer time perspective, and it is a necessary defence that they do. Creative arts are difficult to programme; an over-emphasis on means, ways and deadlines may be counter-creative. After all if Michelangelo had known how long it would take to paint the ceiling of the Sistine Chapel, would he have ever started? But there is a further twist to these different time perspectives as between design and production. This is that design do in fact generally have deadlines; they just overrun them, thereby making difficulties for those who come later in the chain.

To enlarge this last point a little, for any major design of a new product or model there will probably be a date from which customers are supposed to be able to buy it, and salesmen will eagerly take orders 'up the line' (for deliveries on or after this date even though the model may not yet be in production). Behind this sales date, is a manufacturing lead time, which may in fact be inadequate anyway since the product concerned is new. Preceding this manufacturing lead time is an engineering methods and perhaps tooling up period, and the design deadline is prior to this. So when designers overshoot they are putting pressure on production engineers and those who organise production itself, so their delinquencies are much resented. It is made worse by the fact that usually there can be 'no turning back' because the new model is already advertised and often sold.

Another tendency which designers have, again much resented by production managers, is the wish to slip in extras. A designer who realises that some further embellishment is possible (or perhaps some error retrieval is necessary) will often try to effect this even though the item concerned is already in production. And, of course, from a designer's point of view this is totally rational. An improvement is an improvement whether you think of it in June or April (though it does make a difference if production started in May). The other bane for production managers is new products whose specifications are incomplete, typically in the sense of items, dimensions or tolerances missing from the machine drawings. Again, this is quite understandable from a design point of view: designers are people who conceive of new products, draw them, model them and do all the relevant calculations. But they are creating something, not starting with a finished product they can measure. And again the designer's primary struggle is to get from an idea in his mind and a set of calculations to a three-dimensional artifact. Whereas the primary concern of those who come later in the chain is to have something which can be made with ease, perhaps in large numbers, and to a budget.

As with the sales-production relationships there are all sorts of differences of attitude and expectation, emphasis and priority, leading in different directions. It is not a question of personal or particular antagonisms. Having said this, the problem is well known in manufacturing industry and yet there is seldom any provision for it. The plan is based on the assumption that nothing will go wrong, in a situation where something frequently does.

Personnel

The personnel function is interesting for the study of interdepartmental relations in a different way. It is not involved in a hostile or especially controversial relationship with any other department in particular, as are sales, design and production. It suffers from a more pervasive problem of being perceived as marginal. When corporate leaders make resounding statements on the lines of 'Our greatest resource is people', they do not really mean it, it is said for effect. Personnel does not make anything, or sell anything, and does not count the money: this is its problem.

The problem is confounded by two others. Personnel departments owe their origins to paternalistic, wrong-righting, do-gooding attitudes which are today at least unfashionable if not inappropriate. This idea could be expressed in a more general, and at the same time more politically pointed, way by saying that the personnel function in part exists to bridge the disparity of interests between owners and employees.

The second ramification is that there is a lot of variation among the people who staff personnel posts. The range is from managers with character and experience but without formal qualifications to sophisticated graduates with additional professional training. In some companies personnel is quite explicitly a resting place for managers 'burned out' in more exposed jobs, for ex-production controllers or older production managers who find 'the front line' too pressurised. In others personnel is a high ranking function, represented at board level, and staffed by very professional people.

To these general considerations one must add changes over time, and particularly changes incumbent on the 1980-plus recession. In the 1960s and 1970s personnel managers were often seen as people having an important, even dramatic, role in the company because of their hoped-for ability to avert strikes, stem the tide of industrial action and conduct knife-edge pay negotiations. After 1980 these activities became much less salient, and many a young graduate recruited in the 1970s to handle recruitment, training and management development found himself or herself principally concerned with redundancy packages in the 1980s.

What is interesting is the variety of often enterprising ways in which personnel managers have responded to these challenges. As a function personnel has been dealt a weak hand, but played well. In the most general sense personnel departments have become experts in servicing people. Line managers do it in an *ad hoc* way, with an eye to immediate convenience and often with a short time perspective. Personnel departments do it systematically. They administer pay and pension schemes, and run welfare facilities. They keep records, systematise recruitment, standardise application forms, keep tabs on employees and know for what they are eligible and when. They represent a kind of link between the company and society, particularly with society's education system and training institutions. They know the rules for hiring apprentices and what apprentices are entitled to; they know where to send foremen for training, and about job opportunity and retraining schemes. They understand how and where to recruit new generations of managers, and are practised in selection techniques, and 'milk round' interviews.

Another dimension is that it is personnel departments which respond to industrial and industrial relations legislation. Personnel managers know what the law says on safety matters and investigating accidents. They participate in collective bargaining and referee grievance procedures. They understand more systematically than line managers the procedures for hiring and, above all, dismissing employees, and the stages that have to be gone through. All this represents a formidable body of procedural knowledge.

There is another way of looking at it. If there were no personnel departments, many of these responsibilities would be discharged by production managers. Yet production managers have too many other pressures to do these things systematically or on a large scale. So when it comes to systematic recruitment, or redundancy schemes, or the need to organise training across the board, or to institute measures for management development, personnel managers come into their own.

The marginality to which we referred at the outset is probably one factor in the self-conscious professionalism of much personnel management. Personnel management has its own techniques and procedures and these serve the ends of professional identity as well as good administration. So that personnel managers usually view these instruments – selection and recruitment measures, job descriptions, training manuals, job analysis, employee appraisal, schemes for monitoring the progress of young graduates and for personal management development – as 'good things' in their own right, a part of good personnel practice.

There are two further ways in which personnel managers sometimes contribute to their companies and externalise their claim to a distinctive competence at the same time. The most basic is that personnel managers may see themselves as specialists in 'the human side of enterprise'. They may feel, that is, that they have a better understanding of human relations, communication, motivation and how to handle people and their problems. It follows from this that some are ready, indeed eager, to share this understanding in the sense of counselling colleagues and helping individual managers to overcome problems in the human relations or industrial relations area.

The second and related point is that some personnel managers pursue a definitely proactive policy. In large and, particularly, centralised companies, all the rules, conditions and procedures may be promulgated by head office, and be well-known and understood. In such cases the administration of the various systems referred to earlier will be more routine, and typically delegated to subordinates and clerical staff. Such situations open up the possibility of a proactive stance where the personnel manager looks for issues or problems to whose solution personnel skills may contribute.

Purchasing

In this connection of inter-departmental relations the purchasing function offers a perhaps unexpected interest. It can be viewed both on its own terms and from the standpoint of production.

At first sight, it might be thought that, however necessary the purchasing function may be as a *sine qua non* for manufacturing, its role in the organisation must be quite uncomplicated. Not so. Purchasing is often at the centre of a complex set of demands and expectations, some of them contradictory.

First, the finance department has an interest in what the buyers do. Most obviously it wants materials and components to be purchased cheaply. But there is more to it than this. Finance is interested in the financial stability of suppliers (and whether they can be kept waiting for their money without bankrupting them). Indeed finance has an interest in the terms and timing of any deal. It matters for cash flow purposes when an order is placed, and for how much, and when payment has to be made. Finance tends to favour several small orders, paid for piecemeal, rather than one big order to a supplier. And if a big order is made finance will expect buyers to go for a discount, and if it is not forthcoming they will want to know why.

Then purchasing often has an important, and constraining, relationship with design and production engineering. Although the materials and components which purchasing buys are bought for production, they are not always bought on the orders of production. In many cases it is designers or production engineers who declare what is to be bought, establish the technical specifications for required components, and even name or recommend particular suppliers prized for their quality and suitability.

The expectation of the typical production manager is again somewhat different. While he is concerned with quality and price, his main consideration is availability: he wants components in the company, on the shop floor, at the right time for particular manufacturing jobs. So that while engineers pressurise buyers on technical standards and quality issues, production managers pressurise them to meet manufacturing-start deadlines.

Even sales may sometimes have an interest in what purchasing is doing (purchasing, after all, is only sales backwards). There are endless inter-linkings in the business world, such that salesmen may see an advantage of a tactical kind in placing an order here rather than there — with a potential customer, or a customer's affiliate, or sub-contractor, or partner.

In short, then, the buyer is often surrounded by a set of contradictory demands where finance want it cheap, the engineers want it perfect, the salesman seeks some tactical advantage and the production manager wants it now. Buyers, of course, have their own professionalism. They tend to see themselves as specialists in negotiation. They are also inclined to cheapness, and like to 'shop around' for better terms (which production managers hate, fearing some unanticipated problem with any untried supplier). More generally buyers like 'a good deal', not just in terms of base price but with regard to terms and discounts, free delivery, subsidised warehousing, deferred payment and so on. Good buyers also pride themselves on market and product knowledge: on anticipating gluts and shortages, predicting price trends, knowing the range of suppliers, knowing about potential new suppliers ready to enter the market, and about developments in materials or methods which may open up alternatives for their company. Buyers of the old school are also good at maintaining relations with principal suppliers such that they can demand favours — rush orders, deliveries at short notice, preferential treatment when there is a scarcity and deferred payment when there is a cash flow problem.

In other words, buyers like room for manoeuvre and scope to deploy their talent. There are two principal threats to this. One is from designers and engineers who make the technical specifications so tight that the buyer has little choice but to go to the supplier proposed by the engineer. The other restriction is from production managers who are so insistent in their demands for timely deliveries that they convert the buyer into an expediter, who spends his day on the phone to suppliers urging faster and faster deliveries.

Buyers are not in fact helpless before such restrictions, and there are ways in which they can sanction engineers and production managers. It is possible to query specifications and appeal to higher authority, play-off design and production against each other, decline to use personal contacts to get production managers out of a jam, point to cheaper sources and ask finance to intervene, and there is also the trick of turning procedures back on others. So that, for instance, a buyer agrees to implement a late order or an uneconomically small order, but requests a written statement from production that they are prepared to pay a premium rate or bear the expense of special delivery.

As we pointed out in discussing organisation charts in Chapter 1, the purchasing department is sometimes under the direct control of a higher production manager. There is clearly a justification for this, in that it gives production the control to guarantee the availability of purchased items. This means that any disruption of the manufacturing programme is much less likely, and that is a very tangible gain. On the other hand there is a price to be paid for converting the purchasing department into a group of expediters. It undermines their professionalism and militates against the qualitative role of purchasing in respect of negotiation, innovation, and market intelligence. The present trend is towards having purchasing departments which are hierarchically independent of production.

In another country

In discussing these issues of the identity of different management functions and the relations between them we have drawn on a variety of sources going beyond the particular research study which dominated Chapters 1 and 2. At the same time we have written very much with reference to Britain, and to a lesser extent with reference to the USA. Several of these issues are somewhat different in West Germany, and it will add another perspective to point up some of these.

First, the status relativities as between these various management functions are somewhat different in Germany, and such status considerations are less pronounced anyway. Finance is not a high prestige function in German firms, and indeed there is no real equivalent in Germany to our qualified accountant. There the book-keeping functions tend to be discharged by senior clerical workers, and the higher functions of financial management and control by graduates in business economics. Sales is a high status function, as in Britain, though sales and marketing are less Americanised. They are viewed in Germany, that is to say, in a more pragmatic, matter of fact way: a salesman goes out armed with technically detailed brochures, he will be very familiar with the performance characteristics of the product (and is more likely to be an engineer by training), and (at least in good times) the rest is expected to follow. Production is a higher status function in Germany than in Britain, and all the technical functions enjoy higher standing. In Germany design is often named as the *prima donna* function. The standard word for describing design in German is *schöpferisch* (creative) which Germans produce apparently without tongue in cheek.

On the whole, there is probably less rivalry between different departments in German firms, especially among the technical departments or those relating to production. The general point is that the character of

German management is much more explicitly technical anyway, and this tends to produce a unifying effect. To this should be added the fact that for the last thirty years Germany has had a more successful economy than Britain – higher productivity, faster growth, greater personal wealth – and in a situation where everyone has been winning, friction is less likely. There is also a particular point concerning the range of technical functions which is that qualification levels among managers there are higher and more uniform. Just about everyone in these technical functions, including production, has one or other of two standard engineering qualifications. It is also noticeable that German managers take a more holistic view of the non-commercial side of the firm, so that if one asks a production manager if he has always worked in production he is quite likely to reply yes and then detail a series of jobs in production planning, engineering and quality control. One reason why German production managers criticise design less is that many of them are ex-designers.

The nature of personnel management is rather different in West Germany. The personnel manager there conceives his job much more strongly in legal and procedural terms. Personnel management is much more about applying industrial legislation and in particular the legislation on co-determination (worker representation). There is less emphasis on the instruments of personnel practice, and more on the basic exigencies of recruitment and training. German personnel managers at company level are seldom involved in wage negotiations: this all happens at a higher level between employers' associations and trade unions. And in our view German personnel managers are less likely to act in the proactive way described earlier in connection with their British counterparts.

We argued earlier the importance of informal trading and manoeuvre in the regulation of these relationships between departments in Britain and the USA. This is less evident in German companies as well, even allowing for the fact that it is not easy for an outsider (and foreigner) to identify such practices. When one asks German managers leading questions along the lines of 'what really happens?' and 'what do you do if . . .?' one tends to get apparently unselfconscious answers like 'we have a committee to deal with this', 'it's covered by article 625 of the works council act', or 'it would not happen'. This relative absence of informal dealing, not to mention pure intrigue, is also noticeable in our experience in Swedish companies. It may well be that the Anglo-Saxon countries have developed a flair for organisational politics and the view that informal arrangements are the expression of individualism.

Summary

This chapter has dealt with the identity which various management functions construct and the relationships between them. We began with the general proposition that management functions are differentiated not only by task but by centrality, and sometimes by prestige considerations. We drew on various American studies to show how the departments of a company may be viewed as sub-units with a specialised competence, engaging in rivalry and special pleading. We went on to suggest that in some of the classic cases including the sales-production relation and the design-production relationship there are good extrinsic reasons for tension in the sense of real differences of interest. Next we took the personnel function as a test-case of a more marginal management function, analysed its ambiguities and suggested ways in which personnel management in Britain has responded to these. We considered the purchasing function as a case of a department at the receiving end of multiple and contradictory pressures, and showed some of the responses, personal and organisational. Finally we have drawn attention to some of the differences in Germany, where practices are more formal and legalistic, but status relativities are not so poignant. In short they make good engineers but bad intriguers.

Notes

1 A disproportionate number of managing directors have a sales or finance background according to a British survey: Charles Margerison, 'How Chief Executives Succeed', *Human Resource Development*, vol. 4, no. 9, 1980.
2 For data on the relatively low pay of (British) production managers see R.W.T. Gill and K.G. Lockyer, *The Career Development of Production Managers in British Industry*, Bradford Management Centre, 1978. Report to the joint CBI/BIM Advisory Panel on Management Education.
3 More of this British research on production management as a 'cinderella function' is summarised in Peter Lawrence, 'Operations Management: Research and Priorities', report to the Social Science Research Council, May 1983 (also available from the University of Loughborough library).
4 For a more sustained analysis of the technical culture in West Germany see S.P. Hutton and P.A. Lawrence, *German Engineers: the Anatomy of a Profession*, Oxford University Press, 1981.
5 This idea that the organisation leader's primary task is to represent and establish the values of the organisation is developed in Philip Selznick,

Leadership in Administration, University of California Press, 1957.
6 Philip Selznick, *TVA and the Grass Roots*, University of California Press, 1953.
7 For the famous 'who hates whom' in British industry table see K.G. Lockyer and Steven Jones, 'The Function Factor', *Management Today*, September 1980.

Further reading

M. DALTON, *Men Who Manage*, Wiley, New York 1959, for a fascinating account of cabals, coalitions and intrigue in American companies, as well as an analysis of line-staff conflict.
P.A. LAWRENCE and R.A. LEE, *Insight into Management*, Oxford University Press, 1984, has chapters on personnel, purchasing, production, and sales, all of which deal with the interface problem.
P.A. LAWRENCE, 'Personnel Management in West Germany: Portrait of a Function', report to the International Institute of Management, West Berlin, July 1982 (also available from the University of Loughborough library) offers a general account of personnel management in German companies from a British viewpoint.
K.G. LOCKYER and STEVEN JONES, 'The Function Factor', *Management Today*, September 1980; this short article is a must for a fast mapping of interdepartmental antipathies in British industry.

Discussion questions

1 What would you do as managing director to promote harmonious co-operation between sales and production?
2 Would you expect the maintenance department to be:
   (a) well regarded by other managers?
   (b) a high status function?
3 How might a production manager seek to maintain the co-operation of all the sections and departments upon whom he depends?
4 Imagine you had a newly formed personnel department in a medium sized company: what would you do to get your department accepted?
5 What is the case for and against placing the purchasing function under the control of a higher production manager?

4

Industrial relations

On the quayside at Helsinki harbour there is a scruffy little kiosk selling coffee and snacks. As well as displaying a price list it has on view a list of famous politicians – Valéry Giscard d'Estaing, Leonid Brezhnev, Harold Wilson, and so on – who have allegedly supped there. This communication is intriguing precisely because it is unexpected (these names would not be out of place in the register at the Grand Hotel). The present chapter has something of the same quality: it does not run true to type, it puts the emphasis in a different place and challenges some accepted views.

The standard offering on industrial relations is about what is usually called 'the British system of industrial relations' – number, structure and organisation of trade unions; relevant legislation; pay bargaining systems; and probably some analysis of the cause and distribution of strikes. We are not going to follow this line here, for two reasons. First, there are good discussions of such topics in other books. Second, from the point of view of 'management in action' the standard treatment leaves out a lot of happenings and contingencies that impinge on the real work of managers. We also aim to change the emphasis by arguing that strikes are relatively unimportant, that industrial relations incidents may be classified in a number of ways, although some operational generalisations are still possible.

Strikes in their place

There is an optical illusion quality about strike figures: they are so large, it is difficult to imagine any place of work being unaffected. Even when these figures are trimmed a bit by being expressed in terms of population units, they still come out large. Virtuous, peaceable Sweden, for example, lost 49 working days through strikes for every 1,000 employed persons each year throughout a period of growth and prosperity from the mid-1960s to the mid-1970s.[1] The corresponding statistic for Britain was 775, and for Canada 1,849 (which gives the superficial impression that Canadians worked for a day and then struck for two!).

In fact it is better to think of the number of days worked rather than the number of days lost. When the equation is put this way it becomes clear that from the standpoint of any particular manager a strike in his own works in the near future is unlikely (statistically improbable). It is rather like the road death figures. While it is true that some 7,000 people die on Britain's roads each year, the chance that any individual will get killed on his way to work tomorrow is pretty slight. So our first contention is that the importance of strikes, or our impression thereof, is inflated by the literature, the media and the way the figures loom out. In fact, strikes are not a major *direct* contingency for most managers in Britain.

There are perhaps two qualifications to make. First, one should exempt from the above contention a few particularly strike-prone industries, say docks and the car industry. Second, for process industries working on near continuous production, where, that is, the plant is either properly manned and running, or not manned, not running and producing nothing, then the disruptive effect of strikes is to be feared particularly.[2]

Another impression about strikes which needs to be dispelled is the view that they 'strike without warning', like cloudbursts or earthquakes. This sometimes happens, or rather, an unpredictable incident triggers off a strike, but often in a situation of smouldering grievance. On the other hand, there is often a predictable element. Strikes about pay occur in the bargaining season: the strike takes place in the run up to the company or industry or government making a pay offer, to put pressure on them to pitch it higher, or it occurs when an offer has been made which workers or their representatives view as inadequate. In some industries again, strikes are quite literally seasonal: air traffic controllers and cross channel ferry workers strike in the summer; coal-miners and power workers strike in the winter.

This impression that strikes 'strike out of the blue' tends to be encouraged by companies themselves, who do not seem to plan for strikes. Though an individual company cannot predict the future with any certainty, it will have certain indicators. A company will know, for instance, if it had any strikes last year; it will know in the light of its own experience at what time and in relation to what issues a strike is most likely; it will know what production it has lost through strikes over the last several years. Quite straightforward pieces of information of this kind could influence production plans, delivery promises, stock-holding policies and the planned through-put of work very sensibly, but they do not seem to do so.

A third impression which needs to be modified is the idea that strikes produce a maelstrom of frenetic activity, especially on the management side, with all-night negotiations with ACAS and media appearances every half hour. Not so. This is only true for some strikes, coming under recognisable headings. Strikes which affect the comfort and convenience of the general public (power, water, transport, petrol deliveries, for instance) evoke a strong response from government as well as employers. Really bitter strikes to the death over union recognition, plant closure or industry contraction usually involve principles going beyond the interests of those immediately concerned and receive a lot of media attention; and the same might be claimed for 'political strikes' aimed at challenging some legislative initiative or policy stance by government. On the other hand there are many strikes in manufacturing industry that do not have the slightest interest for the general public and receive scant attention from the media.

The extent to which managers simply 'sit out' strikes is also underestimated by the general public. Perhaps it will help to bring it into focus to say that most strikes in Britain are unofficial (not officially recognised by the union to which the striking employees belong), and some of them are 'wildcat'. It is surprising how many of these strikes either do not have a great effect, or simply burn themselves out. Consider in this connection the first three strikes we directly encountered in doing the case studies in British companies.

The first was a strike by a small group of workers on a car assembly line. Their grievance was that carelessness by other workers higher up the line was making their job more complicated and meant they had to work faster; their work was picking any loose oddments that should not be there out of the cars at the end of the production line. These workers struck for an hour, were rewarded by a grievance-airing session with a senior production manager, who obliquely threatened to have their job time-studied while offering to tell other production workers not to leave so much rubbish in the cars, and back they went to the assembly line.

The second strike was an official strike by maintenance workers in support of a pay claim. The general manager of the works concerned said it would make little difference, and that some middle manager with technical skills would do any repairs which were vital to maintain production.

The third incident was a wildcat strike by delivery drivers at a large mass production plant. They struck, without warning, over a safety issue in the loading area, and walked off (on a Thursday afternoon, just after they had been paid). The production manager responsible for this area of the works was informed, went to the site and solved the safety issue, then went back to his office to continue a meeting and was told three-quarters of an hour later that the drivers had resumed work.

These three strikes may not be typical, but they are in a sense chosen at random. And they do serve to redress the balance of popular impression by showing that strikes may occur which are short-lived, are not particularly disruptive, and are 'solved' by management inaction.

This exercise of moderating the popular view of strikes also sets the scene for the rest of the chapter. Our conviction is that from the standpoint of general and production managers in British companies, directly experienced strikes are a relative rarity, but that there is often a steady stream of industrial relations questions and grievances, which seldom get to the strike stage, but which demand the time, attention, foresight and initiative of managers for their prevention or resolution.

Not by bread alone

In the flux of industrial relations questions handled by production managers issues directly relating to pay are a minority. After all, when the rates have been set there is not very much to do until negotiating time looms up again. So questions and grievances about pay tend to operate 'at the edges': workers will query the extras — the bonus, or the shift work supplement, or the calculation of how much they should have earned that week, or whether or not an allowance has been made for a machine breakdown, or why so much tax has been deducted this week, or how the devil can a decent wage be earned when all the 'good jobs' are going to some other section. But the basics of pay are only challenged intermittently.

Instead a fascinating variety of issues and questions are raised: about safety (a good one this because it is more important to workers than managers, but managers have to take it seriously), working conditions, the interpretation of company policy, sub-contracting, promotion prospects, the quality of supervision, demarcation, overtime working (its allocation and timing rather than the rates) and the distribution of tasks. And no matter how many headings there are, by content or subject of grievance, many incidents will still arise that will not fit easily under any of them.

It will be helpful to discuss and illustrate some of these staple items, as well as giving examples of the unclassifiable. We will then develop the idea that industrial relations issues can be classified in a variety of ways, and not simply by cause or content. Following this we will suggest and illustrate some operating generalisations, and round off with a sideways look at industrial relations in West Germany.

Demarcation

Demarcation means putting boundaries round jobs, so that they can only be done by people trained or at least appointed to do them, and not by workers from another trade, section, job classification or skill level. Concern with demarcation tends to be more prevalent in manufacturing than in the service sector, and in the public sector rather than the private, and it reaches its acme in very traditional occupations such as ship-building.

From the viewpoint of the employee, it is both rational and irrational depending on what one chooses to emphasise. In so far as demarcation introduces inefficiencies and frustrates the purposes of management it is irrational for workers to pursue it; other things being equal it makes it less likely that the company will thrive and prosper, which is in the employees' interest. On the other hand, demarcation serves to protect jobs, in the aggregate and in the particular. To insist that only riveters can do the riveting, for instance, will tend to keep up the number of riveters, and protect other groups of workers (since riveters will not do anything but riveting).

In companies where demarcation is in theory taken seriously it may still be modified in practice. One of the medium-term war aims of many production managers in demarcated works is to get workers themselves to ignore demarcation and cross the lines, at least when it is helpful – it pleases management, speeds up a job, avoids a shortage or a bottleneck. The sort of situation in which workers come to do this is where two conditions coincide. First, they perceive no threat to their short-term or material interests – no redundancies are expected, there are plenty of orders and no need to spin work out. Second, it happens where the supervisor or production manager concerned is seen as a good guy, one that workers want to help. Indeed, this is the pay-off for many old-style production managers who live by the golden rule and respect their workers' economic interests and human worth. Such managers may end by commanding a loyalty beyond the call of (demarcated) duty.

Friction in the form of industrial relations incidents inspired by demarcation considerations tends to arise in two ways. The first and most common is that someone, a supervisor or production manager, orders or allows someone to do something, not with the intent of undermining the demarcation system, but just to get a job done in the short term. To give a trite example, an engineering manager interviewed in the course of the study complained at having got into trouble with the union by putting a new bulb in his desk light (only maintenance workers change light bulbs): he did not mean to strike a blow at demarcation, he just wanted a light bulb. To give a more complex example at another company in the study, a charge-hand in one section needed a tool made up, the tool-room claimed not to be able to do it quickly enough, so the charge-hand had it made up by a resourceful mate in another section. This led to a demarcation protest by shop stewards on the grounds that only the tool-room is allowed to make tools, and the fact that the job had been done by a third party section simply added insult to injury. The production manager responsible investigated the incident, took depositions, reported back to the shop stewards, and gave assurances. The charge-hand had the paradoxical experience of being reprimanded by his boss for flouting demarcation lines and being congratulated by the MD for his initiative in keeping his section working with the needed tool.

The second way in which friction may arise is where management takes the initiative in a move to eliminate demarcation — but then it backfires. The usual move is for management to trade the removal of some line of demarcation for something else — a slightly better pay rise, a productivity deal, a concession on some other issue. In one of the companies in the study the works director had initiated the end of demarcation between welders and profile cutters (the latter cut sheet metal to shape with a high intensity torch flame). Subsequently he requested that the welders in this section would work Saturday morning overtime to clear a backlog, only to be met with a demand that since demarcation had ended the profile cutters would work overtime too. In the end the works director had to climb down and rescind the original end to demarcation. But this story leads to yet another recurrent industrial relations issue, that much loved mine-field, overtime.

Overtime

It is often argued by critics of British industrial life that one long-term problem is that many workers work overtime on a regular basis, they see some overtime as part of the normal working week, and the reward for it as part of the standard weekly pay. The argument goes that this is bad for productivity (workers will spin it out during the day to be sure of overtime rates later), contributes to wage drift (the overtime work is paid for at a higher rate) and indicates a lack of planning on the part of companies who ought to be able to cope with a normal work load in normal working hours. There is some truth in this omnibus criticism, though it should not be taken literally in the simplistic form of the above statement. It does, however, contain the clue to one recurrent line of friction where overtime is concerned.

This is that many workers do work regular amounts of overtime over long periods of time, and then experience financial problems (and much irritation) when overtime working is withdrawn — usually because of a fall-off of orders, contraction of business. When this happens it tends to induce a very trigger-happy industrial relations climate, marked by a strong tendency to divert the aggression and irritation over the loss of overtime income into other channels. In the case discussed in the previous section where a charge-hand is reprimanded for having a tool made up by an assembly section instead of the tool-room, the shop stewards in making their case argued that it was particularly unfair since the charge-hand's section was already working regular overtime but the tool-room was not.

In other words overtime working creates a dependence problem. Whether or not regular overtime working is injurious to the economy, its withdrawal certainly creates problems for particular work groups and those who manage them. But there is an even more intractable problem about overtime, which is that management and workers have a different view of it. It is difficult to get hold of this difference because it is unusual for either side to explicate it: they just do things, and occasionally say things, which imply a different conception of the role and function of overtime.

Let us start with management. They view overtime as a rational resource; it brings the company benefits, but it has to be paid for (in terms of premium rates). At least in theory it can be turned on and off at will by management. It is particularly desirable (to turn it on) when there is a backlog of work or the alternative would be to increase the labour force.

Workers and their representatives do not see it this way. Overtime is generally desirable for the addition to the income it yields, it is an 'economic goody'. As such it should be subject to considerations of fair play and fair shares. So everyone ought to get a crack at the whip. It is unfair for one section or group to work overtime when another does not. Or if overtime is 'rationed' it ought to be passed round in turn in an equitable way. It will be noted that the employee view of overtime, whatever its Christian merits, pays little attention to the particular purpose for which management desires the overtime work. Thus when management say they want the welders to work overtime (because they actually need some welding done) shop stewards may retort that it would make better sense to let the capstan lathe operators come in on Saturday because 'they have not had a turn since before Christmas'.

Strangers to industry would be surprised how often disagreements develop from these opposed views of overtime. In one of the companies in the study, a car firm, management invited workers on the estate car line to work overtime at the coming weekend. The shop stewards responded by suggesting that the offer should be made to workers on the saloon car assembly line since the estate car workers had enjoyed more than their share of overtime recently. Management's retort was that it actually wanted to build estate cars not saloon cars, and the stewards counter-attacked with the argument that it is all semi-skilled work anyway and the saloon car workers would build estate cars just as well!

Sub-contracting as class war

Disagreements about overtime are dreadfully common, but not especially bitter. But disagreements over sub-contracting policy may reach the level of class war. Sub-contracting is where a company passes on some of the work it is contracted to do to smaller firms. Sometimes this is on a finished item basis, as for example when a company which has a contract to supply say a foreign government with 30,000 rifles decides to make 20,000 and have the remaining 10,000 made by some smaller armaments firms, all made to the same specifications, and probably with the big firm's name on them as well. But more often sub-contracting is by component, process or sub-process. Sub-contracting by component is where, for instance, a company that makes bulldozers gets someone else to make the gearbox for them, or a company that makes forklift trucks gets another manufacturer to make the electric motors. Sub-contracting by sub-process is where the dominant firm does most of the work but has some limited operation performed elsewhere. A company producing some metal product, for example, might send out components it has made to be galvanised, or nickel-plated, or chromium plated. Sub-contracting by process is where a company sends some of its work out for the purpose of being processed in a main line way while doing the rest itself. Maybe the company's products require much machining of components: the company does some of this machining itself, and sub-contracts the rest. This is the most incendiary option; after all the sub-contractors who make bulldozer gearboxes or do chromium plating may be regarded as specialists, but the sub-contractors who are picking up what we have called sub-contracting by process work are not doing anything the company cannot do for itself (and is doing). A perfect illustration of the opposing forces occurred with one of the companies in the study.

The company concerned is a mechanical engineering firm in the midlands. It was sub-contracting work from the machine shop to a coterie of small, local firms. The shop stewards objected strongly to this, and demanded and got a meeting with senior management to state their case. The essence of the shop steward case was that the company should not sub-contract work from the machine shop unless or until it was in a position to offer regular overtime working to the machine shop (and then if it still had too much work sub-contracting would be accepted). Note the way the issues of sub-contracting and overtime are interlinked; this interlinking of issues is very common in industrial relations. The case for the prosecution was further strengthened by the stewards claiming that the sub-contractors were all local, they were paying higher rates to their employees, and offering them regular overtime.

At the meeting management came back with a multiple defence, of which the key points were:

1 It would be immoral to take on extra workers to deal with the present work-load and then dismiss them in three or four months' time if work falls off. (Readers will note that it is a particularly neat argument, though wildly specious, in that it enables management to gain moral superiority as really caring for the rights of man.)

2 You have to keep the sub-contractors happy all the time or they will desert you in your hour of need.

3 Sub-contracting is a recognised way of dealing with the fluctuations in demand with which manufacturing companies are confronted (perfectly true) and there is no reason to object to it in this case.

4 Sub-contracting is cheaper because you do not have to pay the overheads (in the ensuing discussion management was challenged to produce its figures in support of this claim and declined).

5 We are management, and we know best.

Apart from lining up all the for and against arguments in an ideal-type way, the discussion was interesting in two other ways. First, the workers' representatives made very little headway against the management position and got no concessions. None the less they appeared in a certain sense satisfied and commented that they were glad to have had such a frank discussion. It may not be obvious to outsiders, but there is an element of victory in forcing a group of senior managers into a meeting and tongue-lashing them for two hours. There is also an element here of the fact that workers like meetings: having an exchange with senior management is, after all, a lot more fun than working the lathes.

Second, at the end of the meeting the leader of the management team took the author on one side to explain what it was 'really' all about. If the company stopped sub-contracting, and offered overtime to the machine shop, then the rest of the works would go slow until it got overtime as well. This communication is interesting in that it represents a wider consideration, namely, that there is often a hidden agenda in industrial relations, that what they talk about is not the real issue. The corresponding communication from the shop steward side might well have been: we know they won't stop sub-contracting, but we've made it more difficult for them to decline to replace workers who leave.

The unpredictable meets the unclassifiable

We suggested earlier that some of the incidents that arise in industry do not fit neatly under any heading, but are real enough and still engage the time and energy of 'managers in action'. Just to give the flavour of the unexpected we will describe incidents from three companies, pointing the occasional moral.

In company one there is a tradition, and tradition is important in industrial relations, that welders who work on galvanised materials are provided with free milk, the idea being that the milk will somehow allay any galvanised impurities that are inhaled. This company then acquired a new metal spraying apparatus, and the workers who were to use this also demanded free milk on the basis of a putative health risk. The manufacturing director took the employees' implicit health concern seriously and contacted the supplier of the metal sprayer for advice. The supplier did indeed have the answer, in the shape of personalised ventilators – these are rather like miners' helmets with compressed air cylinders on top which blow clean air into the face of the worker who can then not inhale any spray-polluted air. The employees tried these but rejected them on the grounds that they gave the wearer a stiff neck. They returned to their original demand for free milk, after the manner of the 'galvanised welders'. When it became clear that the manufacturing director would not give in on the milk ('it's been the bane of my life') the workers concerned retaliated by ostentatiously wearing masks of the type the painters wore. This is as much about saving face as saving lungs, but saving face is important in industrial relations.

Company two. A machine operator messes up a job which has to be scrapped. He is told off by his foreman. Subsequently he engineered a discussion of the incident with another foreman who took an ameliorative 'don't worry, not your fault, it could happen to anyone' view. What this second foreman did not know, however, was that his remarks were recorded on a hidden tape-recorder; the employee then started to try to make political capital from them, suggesting that his original reprimand had been unjustified. How would you handle that one?

Company three had trouble with tea breaks (no account of industrial relations in England is complete without a dispute about tea breaks). In this works ten minutes was allowed for the tea break, but over time this ten-minute break had expanded to half an hour. Part of the explanation was that the works had no canteen, and that tea and snacks were purveyed by a tea lady with a mobile trolley which she would station in the middle of the one (large) workshop. A lot of the thirty minutes was spent walking to and from the trolley and more particularly in queuing. Management's 'final solution' was to have three phased tea breaks with the tea trolley positioned at three different spots within the workshop, thus reducing walking and queuing time. The only problem was that one group of workers were boycotting the system by taking their (thirty-minute) break at the old time. The manager in charge of the workshop finally brought them into line by threatening to take the issue up with outside union officials. Again strangers to industry might be surprised by the fact that it is often *management* that threatens to bring in trade union officials.

Classifying industrial relations issues

A key part of the argument so far is that industrial relations incidents are highly variable; it is not just about strikes over pay, but about a myriad of other things including some recurrent themes such as demarcation and overtime and safety issues. It is possible to push home this point by showing that industrial relations incidents can be classified in a number of ways, viz:

1 By content, subject, or cause, with the emphasis being on the empirical variety.

2 By degree of seriousness. It is important to take on board the fact that many of these issues are not at all serious and will burn themselves out or go away in the fullness of time. The effect of media coverage, and some executive pronouncements, is to give the general public an over-august view of what industrial relations is all about.

3 Industrial relations issues can be classified by outcome:
  who wins and loses
  is it a compromise solution
  or stalemate
  or postponement
  or no decision
  or one of those miraculous situations where everyone wins.
The point to emphasise is that many industrial relations incidents end in stalemate, (indefinite) postponement and indecision: a clear compromise is rather dramatic.

4 These incidents may also be classified on an inside v. outside basis; in terms, that is, of the involvement or non-involvement of outside agencies especially outside union officials. A conflict between managers and shop stewards, however acrimonious, is all in the family, and the contestants know they are going to have to live with each other afterwards. As soon as any outside person or agency is drawn in, a line is crossed. This is both qualitative, and an escalation.

5 These industrial relations issues may be classified as of routine or of crisis origin. We tend to think of the substance of industrial relations as being all crisis, but this is not so. A lot of the issues are not crises, and are not raised when they occur/arise, but routinely at some scheduled meeting. As was argued in Chapter 2, most medium-sized British companies do have some works committee or assembly at which such issues may be raised by worker representatives.

Operational generalisations

So far we have stressed the heterogeneity of industrial relations issues and the variety of ways in which they may be classified. In the last few pages we will pursue the opposite tack and suggest some generalisations about the conduct of industrial relations. These observations are directed more to management (especially its younger, less experienced representatives) than to the representatives of workers. The latter are not conspicuously in need of operating tips but their opposite numbers in management sometimes are.

Complication

Most industrial relations incidents are more complicated than they appear at first sight. It is important to grasp that the accounts given by either side are likely to be at least incomplete (suppressing key bits of information) and are sometimes downright misleading. This dictum is especially relevant for management in that the manager, almost by definition, may only become involved when the issue has reached a certain stage or gained a certain degree of seriousness. What one is told at this point may be only the tip of the iceberg. Consider, for example, the following case.

The author once sat in on a meeting between a production superintendent and his several foremen in which the superintendent propounded the terms of a recently concluded productivity deal. The foremen seemed at first disappointed, then downright hostile, and finally wearily resigned. At first sight this was a failure of managerial leadership or lack of solidarity among 'them', but consider the (painstakingly unpacked) background.

The company concerned had a few weeks earlier concluded a new pay deal with its employees. Part of the rise that had been granted was to be offset by a productivity deal, the terms of which were to be worked out after the pay rise. The company had begun by inviting the foremen to suggest key elements for this productivity deal. The two things most strongly recommended by the foremen were first that workers turning up for the night shift, but who had culpably missed an earlier day shift, should be sent home; and second, that management should have the right to start an assembly line even if it were inadequately manned, and have a period of grace in which to complete the manning. These two points were taken on board by management and duly presented to the shop stewards as part of the productivity deal: they were rejected categorically. Management then rethought its position, and put together a new (relatively inoffensive) set of demands, without consulting the foremen. These were duly accepted by the shop stewards and were enshrined in the productivity agreement. The foremen were a little disenchanted to hear the terms of the final agreement, while having considerable personal respect for the manager who propounded them at the briefing session.

Unconnected issues will be brought together for bargaining purposes

At first sight this connecting of the unconnected is irrational, and both sides purport to be surprised by it, yet from a bargaining point of view it is good tactics. If after all you are going to give way on x why not try to make a gain on y; if something is being demanded why not make an unrelated counter-claim, it may be the best chance you are going to have. The trick is working out in advance what the counter-claim might be, and deciding whether the price is worth paying.

Consider the following example. In one company in the study there was a general backlog of work as the result of an earlier industry-wide official strike in support of a pay claim. This backlog was particularly acute in the welding section, so management summoned representatives of the welders, explained the situation, and politely invited the welders to work overtime. The representatives agreed the request was entirely reasonable and agreed to pass it on to their colleagues with an appropriate recommendation. The following day, however, the representatives reported back that the welders were only prepared to work overtime if a concession were made on the timing of the working day.

Some time earlier the employees had requested that the working day should start at 7 a.m. instead of 8 a.m. (and finish correspondingly earlier). Management agreed to the request, but at the same time changed the period of grace from five minutes after the starting time to two minutes after the starting time (i.e. under the new regime anyone coming later than 7.02 would lose a quarter of an hour's pay). The welders made their willingness to work overtime conditional on the re-institution of five minutes' grace from 7 a.m. Management professed itself horrified at the irrationality of these linked issues (and refused to give in) yet the starting time leeway was known to be a grievance. If the management's need for overtime in the welding shop had not re-opened the issue, something else would have done.

Redefinition is the art of presentation

There is a tendency for issues to be redefined in the interest of acceptability in industrial relations. The general pattern is for redefinition to be from the less tangible to the more tangible, from the non-monetary to the monetary. The key, usually, is that neither side can complain about not getting, or losing, things it should not have anyway, so any 'sense of loss' has to be re-defined.

There is, for example, a famous study of a gypsum plant in the American middle-west.[3] At this plant a benign management allowed workers considerable latitude. So long as they did a decent day's work and output targets were met, workers would be allowed to arrive late and leave early, spread out the coffee breaks, take the odd day off, borrow the company's tools and equipment for DIY jobs, steal (modest amounts of) the produce (plaster board), and not bother too much about company rules and regulations. Then a new general manager arrived with a head office exhortation to tighten things up ringing in his ears. The tightening up was effected and caused considerable irritation among the workforce. On the other hand, they could hardly mount a formal protest over not being able to go fishing on weekdays or steal plasterboard from the works. But it did not stop them from striking for a considerable payrise. This phenomenon is known as the monetisation of discontent.

General discontent may give rise to particular grievance

The point has arisen in some of the earlier examples that certain things may predispose a workforce to general discontent which will find a particular expression later. Thus chagrin over the cessation of overtime earnings, fear of possible redundancies, or unease about a takeover, may find expression in over-sharp grievances about, say, safety matters or supervision, or demarcation.

Custom and practice

Custom and practice is a standard, indeed hallowed, phrase in the rhetoric of British industrial relations. It is most often appealed to by representatives of workers as a justification for doing things in a certain way, keeping hold of rights or concessions they already have, or resisting (managerially initiated) change. If it is custom and practice to do it this way rather than that, then there has to be a good reason to change (or a tangible inducement).

Custom and practice clearly has a homely appeal for those who plead it. It represents the way things are now, and have been for a while. One does not need to be clever to understand what it is (only to find ways round it) so it is a little bit the plain man's bulwark against 'clever dicks' from head office, the personnel department or management services section who have thought up yet another privilege disrupting initiative in the name of greater efficiency. In short, custom and practice has to be taken seriously, and is not readily susceptible to frontal attacks.

Management vulnerability will be exploited

Companies which allow anomalies to arise, in payment systems, in the treatment of personnel, in conditions between plants, for example, or which break safety rules, violate agreed procedures, or ignore industrial legislation are rendering themselves vulnerable. Sooner or later the dereliction will be spotted; it may not be the subject of immediate complaint, but sooner or later it will arise as part of an omnibus grievance, a weakness to be exploited, a chance to gain moral superiority, or as a bargaining counter in some other industrial relations dispute.

In one of the companies in the study worker representatives requested an emergency meeting of the safety committee at which they argued that on the previous shift a compressor had blown its safety valve and was, therefore, unsafe. The maintenance manager argued strenuously that he had inspected the compressor and found nothing wrong; he was supported in this view by management colleagues. The worker representatives persisted with the charge and then brought out the *pièce de resistance*: some time ago, before the present maintenance manager was in his post, the compressor had broken down; the previous maintenance manager had repaired it cannibalising parts from another not entirely compatible piece of equipment – the cannibalistic repair had made the compressor unsafe. The maintenance manager had not in fact known any of this.

In other words there are practical and self-interested reasons for managers to 'run a tight ship' in such respects, as well as ethical and professional ones.

The ritual element

Industrial relations clashes, and for that matter procedures, are not (usually) all ritual: they are about real issues which affect and mean something to the parties concerned. But there is often a ritual element in the way they are articulated, presented and pursued. Failure to recognise this may lead managers, typically cast in the reactive role, 'to get it wrong'.

The ritual element takes various forms. These include a tendency for both sides to exaggerate, to overstate the case or over-react to the communications of others. There is the raising of issues, not for their own sake, but for what they may lead to, as bargaining counters, or to gain some tactical advantage. Again, at least on the employee side, there is a certain fondness for procedures and meetings; as was shown in the first two chapters, managers spend a lot of time at meetings, but are not especially fond of them. Employees, on the other hand, tend to find meetings more fun than work. This mild predilection for meetings on the part of worker representatives is also buttressed by the view, referred to earlier, that actually bringing management to a meeting, pinning them down and making them listen, is itself some sort of a gain. Finally, the ritual element includes the need to save face. This may have surprising manifestations.

In one company in the study, for example, a worker had been suspended as a punishment for poor attendance. Aided and abetted by a young shop steward, bucking for re-election it was claimed on the management side, the worker appealed against his suspension. The appeal was in the form of an appearance of the worker, the sympathetic shop steward, and the deputy convenor, before a panel presided over by a senior manager. On encountering this deployment of management strength at the hearing the shop steward lost his nerve and found himself unable to plead the cause of his colleague.

This more or less chance happening thrust the deputy convenor up on to the firing line. The interesting thing was not the content of the convenor's defence, but the way he managed to insinuate that whatever he had to say would be taken seriously. His actual defence, totally unconvincing, was that the worker had been genuinely ill, had sent in a medical certificate to prove it, which the personnel department had then lost; he concluded by demanding an adjournment so that management could investigate this charge!

This testimony was received dead-pan by the management team, the meeting duly adjourned, and the charge was investigated. When the meeting was reconvened the following day the worker's suspension was confirmed, without any further argument, but by then a different kind of justice had been done.

The contrasted world-views of the shop steward and the young graduate

We have picked 'the young graduate' in industry to point up this contrast because he is the most disadvantaged in industrial relations dealings (regarded as a weak link by his managerial colleagues, and as easy meat by shop stewards). The contrast focuses around different views of cleverness and rationality. The prototypical young graduate tends to see cleverness in terms of reasoning ability. What he has derived from higher education, apart from mastery of some particular subject, is the ability to think. He can think logically, analyse, prioritise, even spot *non sequiturs* in arguments presented to him. But these abilities do not constitute a dreadfully strong hand for dealing with shop stewards.

Workers and their representatives tend not to be much impressed by pure reasoning ability, and still less by intellectual virtuosity and formal qualifications. Cleverness is not the ability to spot *non sequiturs* but the ability to get your own way. And when it comes to the means, what is important is facts, circumstantial and procedural, not the logical properties of statements. But the young graduate is not very strong on facts, has not been around long enough to have mastered them, and tends to find it all a bit arid anyway. He also tends to miss the ritual element, takes statements at their face value rather than as encoded political messages, and on occasion does really crazy things like making the best offer first. It usually takes an older manager to see that the best way to stop a shop steward dead in his tracks is to tell him, with half an hour of circumstantial detail, that whatever he wants was tried in 1968 and was a total disaster. Or to put it another way, it is not unusual for one or other party to win in an industrial relations incident, not because they have right on their side, or the benefit of pure reason, but because they have staying power. As in First World War battles, attrition may be a powerful factor.

Scenes from German life

So far the discussion in this chapter has been concerned with industrial relations issues in Britain. It is well known that West Germany has a much better strike record: there are fewer strikes, and fewer working days lost through strike action. What is more, the strikes that do occur are much more likely to be official (called and supported by the relevant trade union), wildcat strikes are much less common and demarcation disputes virtually unknown.

These facts are already well documented, but the study showed something else with regard to Germany. This is that the incidence of all the other industrial relations incidents of the kind discussed in this chapter is much lower as well. Indeed the case studies in German firms offered various illustrations of a remarkably compliant posture on the part of workers and their representatives.

In one of the German firms, for example, a senior production manager decided it would be desirable to end overtime working in the welding section and substitute a shift work system instead in order to cope with a high work load, a proposal which would be highly inflammatory in the typical British firm. The manager concerned discussed it first with the superintendent in charge of the welding section, and then proceeded to a meeting with the chairman of the works council (the approximate equivalent of a senior shop steward in Britain). The chairman listened attentively to the manager's account of the need for the change in terms of greater throughput of work and the company's obligations to customers. At the end of this exegesis the chairman of the works council retorted: 'It is the duty of the works council to oppose shift work, but if it is in the interests of the company . . . .' It was all settled in a quarter of an hour.

In Chapter 2 we illustrated the range of *ad hoc* meetings in which a manager might be involved by citing a company in a northern town cut off by a blizzard. When melting snow put one of the transformers out of action, thereby reducing the supply of electric power, the production manager responded to this contingency by turning out the lights and running most of the machines (in England this would be enough to put NATO on a red alert). Somewhat as an afterthought the manager sought out the works council chairman, hunched over his machine in a darkened shop, and explained the position saying that full power (and lights) would probably be restored by lunch time. The chairman rose with dignity from his work and replied: 'Don't worry, we can live with this.'

To put this contrast a little in perspective, it is only fair to say that there is an organisational-institutional difference too. This is that what complaints and grievances there are in German firms tend to be funnelled very much through the works council which in turn will tend to deal with the personnel department rather than with supervisors or line managers, so that the latter are somewhat shielded. Thus it is not entirely a matter of culture and attitude differences, but also of procedures for responding to worker initiatives. Even so the difference is striking to a foreign observer.

Summary

This chapter has been concerned primarily with the nature of industrial relations in British companies, and has put the emphasis not on 'the system of industrial relations' but on the range of actual issues which working managers confront. We suggested that strikes are in fact of less direct importance than is generally supposed, and that many are surprisingly short-lived as well. The substance of industrial relations questions is rather a variety of other incidents, some recurrent, some highly idiosyncratic. We took three of these recurrent issues — demarcation, disagreements about overtime and sub-contracting — discussed these in more detail and offered actual examples. To this we added some random but real life illustrations of incidents of a less classifiable kind.

From this base we suggested that it is possible to classify industrial relations issues in a variety of ways, and to do this serves the end of better understanding. So that these incidents may be classified not only on the basis of cause and content, but also in terms of their degree of seriousness, the outcome, the routine or crisis nature of their origin, and by whether or not outside agencies, especially external union officials, are involved. This was followed by propounding some generalisations about industrial relations transactions, arguing that the issues are often more complicated than they appear at first sight, that unconnected issues may be brought together for bargaining purposes, that issues are often redefined for tactical reasons, and the transaction often contains a ritual element. In this connection we tried to highlight the different approach of management and workers by looking at the different orientations of the shop steward and the inexperienced graduate manager. Finally we noted that not only is the strike record better in West Germany but that the incidence of industrial relations issues generally is perceptibly lower, a fact which is explained partly in terms of different attitudes but also by procedural differences in which personnel departments have a more central role than in Britain.

Notes

1 These strike figures for various countries are taken from the *Department of Employment Gazette*, vol. 86, no. 11, HMSO, November 1978.
2 This point about the critical nature of strike-stoppages in process plants comes out in Joan Woodward, *Industrial Organisation: Theory and Practice*, Oxford University Press, 1965.
3 The study of the American gypsum plant is written up in Alvin Gouldner, *Wildcat Strike*, Antioch Press, Ohio, 1954.

Further reading

H.A. CLEGG, *The Changing System of Industrial Relations in Great Britain*, Blackwell, 1979. A standard authoritative account, important as a complement to the foregoing chapter.

R. HYMAN, *Strikes*, Fontana, new edition, 1977. Readable and informative.

For other perspectives on shop stewards:

J. GOODMAN and T. WHITTINGHAM, *Shop Stewards*, Pan, 1973.

E. BATSTONE, I. BORASTON and S. FRENKEL, *Shop Stewards in Action*, Blackwell, 1977.

And for a look at the top end of industrial democracy in several countries:

PETER BRANNEN, ERIC BATSTONE, DEREK FATCHETT and PHILIP WHITE, *The Worker Directors*, Hutchinson, 1976.

Discussion questions

1 What does it mean to say that there is a ritual element in industrial relations?
2 How and why are disconnected issues brought together in the practice of industrial relations?
3 Why are overtime, demarcation and sub-contracting recurrent grievance issues?
4 What makes a company vulnerable to disruption through industrial relations incidents?
5 Why are industrial relations better in West Germany?

5

On schedule: a tale of two cultures

It is often important for manufacturing companies to deliver goods to their customers on time, and the struggle to do so engages the attention of production managers and others. There would appear to be marked differences in the extent to which companies achieve this laudable aim of punctual deliveries, and it is also likely that there are differences between countries. Certainly there appears to be such a difference between Great Britain and West Germany, which it will be interesting to explore here.

In fact the present chapter addresses two questions:
1 Why are orders often delivered late?
2 Why is the German performance different from the British one?
But first there are some preliminaries.

Is there a case to answer?

As far as Britain is concerned there is. It has long been popularly held that British companies in general have a poor record on delivery punctuality, and that this is a handicap in export selling. Unfortunately, there is also some hard evidence for this in the form of a survey of international buying and selling embracing sample companies and managers from Britain, France, Italy, West Germany and Sweden.[1] The gist of this study is that buyers in particular were quizzed about their experience and evaluation of the performance of companies from the several countries and of representatives of these companies (principally salesmen of course).

One of the issues explored in this study is precisely that of delivery punctuality. The international sample put Sweden and West Germany top for good delivery performance and Britain bottom (after Italy). Nor, unfortunately, is it simply a question of our being 'done down' by foreigners: there are a number of occasions in the write-up of the study where the consensus verdict is broken down by nation. In many of these instances the severest critics of British faults and failings were the British themselves.

There is also some evidence for Britain considered alone. Colin New has made a general study of the organisation of manufacturing operations in a sample of 158 UK companies, and this study includes an analysis of the delivery performance of a sub-sample of 153 plants.[2] The results do give cause for concern. The 3 per cent who delivered everything on time were matched by another 3 per cent who delivered nothing on time. The author of this study writes:

> 25% of the replying plants reported that less than half their total output (in terms of number of orders) was delivered on or before time. Since the period covered was the year 1975, a year of economic recession for most plants, it is disturbing to contemplate the likely delivery performance in a year of economic boom. Setting the target at the not too ambitious level of 90% satisfaction of customer delivery promises (that is, one in ten orders to be delivered late), 80% of the plants failed to meet target.[3]

The worst is yet to come. It has to be added that the figures are based not on external investigation but on information the firms themselves proffered deriving from their own records. A by-product of this mode of inquiry, noted by its author, is the discovery that:

> Surprisingly, almost two out of five plants definitely stated that they do *not* formally monitor performance against promised delivery dates.[4]

Since the completion of this study Colin New and a colleague, Michael Sweeney, have embarked on another inquiry which involves the researchers themselves going into the co-operating companies and checking contract promises against dispatch notes. While the emphasis of the research has changed to that of trying to identify the problems and devise remedies, the initial report from this study serves to document further the fact of unsatisfactory performance.[5] It would seem that there is a case to be answered.

Is it simple?

Readers may feel that, although the question of delivery punctuality is clearly important, when it comes to causes and remedies there is probably not much to it, just a question of trying a little harder or making sure the workers don't go on strike. We would like to contest this view. Poor delivery performance has a complex aetiology, there are lots of possible and frequently overlapping causes, and it is counter-productive to home-in on some single factor such as strikes. What is more, poor delivery performance is also often complex as a process, with additional reasons. Consider a couple of examples.

A link in the sub-contracting chain

Company A, large and very influential, has given a contract to Company B for a large number of fabricated storage units. Company B sub-contracts seventeen of these to Company C, and it is Company C which is the object of the story. Company C is not to send the units, as and when they are completed, to either Company A (the customer) or Company B (the sub-contractor), but to Company D who will build on something else before sending them on to the customer, Company A. Transportation of the units from Company C to Company D is the responsibility of Company B who has sub-contracted it to Company E.

At the outset all bodes well. An order from Company A is highly desirable. Company B and Company C are geographically close, and their chief executives are on good terms. Company B has already asked for a top level meeting to discuss future co-operation and hoped-for joint orders with Company C. The precise recipient of the sub-contract for the seventeen units is Division X at Company C, whose general manager is a legend in the Group for his drive and forcefulness. What could possibly go wrong?

Company C's actual delivery commitment is to have two units completed every two weeks to be transported to Company D for finishing. Company D is 300 miles away, and Company C has had no prior dealings with it. The first thing that in fact goes wrong is that Company A, who has nominated itself as the supplier of the basic raw material to Companies B and C, sends Company C the wrong raw material. It takes several weeks to sort out this so Company C is now behind schedule without having started, and in delivery terms the customer has torpedoed himself.

Part of the overall agreement is that Company D will send its own inspectors to Company C to check on the quality of 'work-in-progress' on the first pair, to be sure that it will be able to make its contribution at the next stage. It is never clear why, but Company D delayed sending its inspector for seven weeks. Company C is now hopelessly behind schedule through no fault of its own or, at least, as a result of the failures of others.

In these circumstances the general manager at Division X convenes a meeting with his principal subordinates to devise some remedial strategy. Preparing for this meeting he goes through the contract file and finds among the exchange of letters between Company C and Company D that someone at the latter has slipped in a clause changing Company C's commitment from two units a fortnight to two units a week. If this semi-clandestine revision is accepted Company C's difficulty is compounded.

Undeterred the general manager runs his meeting and generates a plan to make up for lost time with a massive dose of overtime working. This meeting is on a Thursday. Later on the same day the shop steward representing the production workers announces an overtime ban and work to rule with effect from the following Monday as a protest against the Company's recent (in their view) inadequate wage offer.

It may be objected that this is an untypical example, with so many parties to the contract, and complications of inter-firm inspection and a nominated supplier to boot. Well, the example is towards the complicated end of the spectrum, but there frequently are a lot of interdependencies in business. Consider anyway a second example, the straightforward attempts of one company to sell something to another.

Some quick profit on the side

In this second case the company concerned, the supplier-seller, processes a natural raw material to produce intermediate foodstuffs. Because it has the contacts and resources of a multi-national it is able to buy competitively, and has the opportunity to resell some of the raw material to a company in Sweden at a profit, a welcome addition to the cash flow. The company hires a cargo ship in advance, and in preparation starts to stock pile the commodity at the relevant port. Here the first difficulty arises in that there is a shortage of storage silos at the port, and silo loading restrictions are also imposed, so that the company is only allowed to load at the weekends and in the evening. Nevertheless the allocated silo is loaded and the chartered cargo ship arrives. At this point it emerges that the silo is defective and cannot discharge its cargo directly into the ship. So the cargo is unloaded on to lorries instead and taken by road to a second port, to which the ship is also diverted. By the time the ship reaches the second port, the dockworkers there are on strike so a further delay ensues. The ship is eventually loaded and sets sail, but by this time the Baltic has frozen and the ship has to dock on the west side of Sweden, though the customer is on the east side (Stockholm). At this stage the captain of the hired cargo ship threatens to sell the cargo unless he is compensated for the demeurage (arising from the delay) in the second port in England (strike-bound). He is pacified, but the cargo then has to be taken across Sweden by lorry to the customer in the east.

These two examples of delivery failure are perhaps more spectacular than the daily average, but they are instructive in some ways. They highlight the dependent position of managers who have responsibility to deliver on time; no would-be punctual deliverer is an island, and in extreme cases the responsible manager, like the snake before the mongoose, foresees disaster and yet is powerless to avert it. There is also a sense in which the examples show the penalty of operating in, broadly speaking, an unfavourable environment, a point to which we will return. The immediate need, however, is to identify some of the recurrent obstacles to delivery punctuality.

What goes wrong?

As we suggested at the outset, there may be a bewildering variety of things going wrong and contributing ultimately to late deliveries.

Give us the tools

Probably the most frequently recurring factor which contributes to poor delivery performance, heralded in the first of the two examples above, is the late arrival of the raw materials or other purchased items in the first place. This in turn may have a variety of causes. First, the buying company may have placed the order late, either through inefficiency, because of a cash flow problem, or because they themselves are at the receiving end of a customer who has changed an order or who wants over-fast delivery. Then there is pure inefficiency on the part of the supplier. It is noticeable that for some suppliers lateness is almost standard: in prosperous times it is, presumably, because they have taken on more work than they can cope with; in a recession they will be spinning out the little they have. A variation on the theme of late delivery of parts or materials from suppliers is when they send the wrong items. People without experience of industry would be surprised how often this happens; in fact the Red Star parcels service thrives on wrong items being sent back to suppliers and right items being expedited. Yet another variation is where the supplier sends the right thing, at the right time, but in the wrong number. There are two possible reasons for this, apart from sheer incompetence. The first is that sending customers (a few) more than they asked for and invoicing them for it is a very painless way of putting up sales (and profits). It is a common practice with small items having a lowish individual value such that the firm on the receiving end will find it easier to just pay for the extra rather than send them back. This over-supplying phenomenon does not pose any problem for the production operation at the buying company, and on occasion it can be downright helpful (what a good thing they sent seventeen instead of twelve: we've lost three and broken two). The accounts department do not like it of course, and the prevalence of over-supplying has decreased since the 1980 recession. The second variation on sending the wrong number is where the supplier sends too few. The usual explanation in this case is that the supplier has more orders than he can cope with, and rather than turn any away or risk losing them by quoting a realistic lead time, he accepts them all and then tries to redeem the situation by sending them all something (enough to keep them happy?) on time, and the rest later. This can cause the buying firm all sorts of problems in the sense of having to manufacture in uneconomical double batches or replicating setting up time.

Finally in this connection is the case where the supplier sends the right thing in the right number at the right time, but there is some defect which renders it unusable. In a lot of cases this will just be poor workmanship or inspection at the premises of the supplier, but there are also occasions when there is a real difficulty about getting the component right, acknowledged on both sides. A good example is castings. Many companies need metal castings for their work and buy them in from a foundry, but here we come to the difficulty. The big foundries supply the big manufacturers, and typically do not want the small orders from lesser firms. These take their business to the smaller foundries which often lack the equipment and sophistication to get it right, or to get it right consistently. It leads to the sort of situation where the foundry responding to an order for seventeen will make twenty-three, reject four themselves, send nineteen, and the purchasing company will reject another three and not have (quite) enough for the product batch for which the castings are intended.

Thou shalt not pass

There are a variety of ways in which the inspection process at a company may contribute to late delivery of finished goods to customers, both wittingly and unwittingly. Let us start at the beginning, with the company's goods inwards inspection, where materials and components from outside suppliers (see previous section) are officially checked-in and inspected. There are three things which may happen at this stage with delaying effects.

The first is that goods inwards inspectors check some item, find it genuinely defective, and reject it. That is their job, but of course a delay then ensues while the supplier sends replacements, or agrees to re-work the original items, or agrees that the buying firm may rectify the items at the supplier's expense.

The second takes us into a grey area. The goods inwards section may reject something because it is 'out of spec' (does not conform to specification). But there may be dispute about whether or not this actually matters. The typical line-up in such disagreements is that of a quality control manager standing by the decision of his goods inwards inspectors, perhaps trying to pull in support from engineers, while a production manager protests that the deviation from specification is quite trivial, has no operating implications, and in any case he needs those parts now for the current manufacturing programme.

The third possibility, and in our experience by far the most common, is that the goods inwards section is simply slow. Bottlenecks are very common in goods inwards, with the result that items needs for manufacture have indeed arrived from the supplier, and are probably perfectly all right, but are languishing in goods inwards awaiting inspection.

At the other end of the process, that is the company's own final inspection of products before they are sent to its customers, the corresponding eventualities may occur. Some products may be found wanting and rejected, they may be rejected on a specificational technicality, or they may simply wait a long time for inspection and clearance. Again it is the last that is probably most common, and it is recognition of this that leads production managers to try to get some operating control of inspection so that they can allocate tasks and prioritise them (see Chapter 1).

There is another twist to the inspection story which should be mentioned. Sometimes the customer sends his own inspectors to the manufacturing company, and on occasion even has inspectors permanently based there. This is common in cases where the customer is a ministry or government department or public authority. In the author's experience, customer inspectors with the majesty of the Secretary of State behind them are to be feared above all (they will eat the seven-course meal and still reject the product). But they are also in the ironic position of in part determining their own delivery punctuality.

New products means new problems

New products, or any special product that the company has not made before, are good candidates for eventual late delivery. The paradox is that, although one knows that teething troubles are to be expected, one does not know what they will be, so there is not much that can be done in advance except expect the worst and allow twice as long as should be necessary. The sort of problems involved in the introduction of new products have been mentioned already in Chapter 3 in the discussion of the design operation, and the relationship between design, engineering and production.

Technical determinism

There are a number of technical and quasi-technical factors which may contribute to poor delivery performance by any given company. The most general of these is that much industrial plant and equipment in Britain is old. The very strong commitment to modernising and replacing plant and machinery which is so obvious in, for example, West Germany, is largely absent in Britain. Indeed a lot of companies in Britain display an inverted pride in having 'a lot of rubbish' on the shop floor and still getting work out of it. What is more, it is not just chief executives far removed from the fray who espouse such sentiments, but production managers themselves often show perverse satisfaction in making do with creaking old machines; it is, of course, a challenge to their resourcefulness.

There is a more general way of putting it. Britain has had more than its share of great engineers and engineering triumphs, but it is not a country that has a strong engineering culture. To take Germany as the contrast again, in that country engineering enjoys higher status and tends to attract more talent, and in business companies more thought, energy and money go into the technical aspects. So that not only is plant and machinery likely to be newer, but there will be a keener interest in machinery lay-outs, materials handling and the whole spectrum of production methods.

To return to something quite specific, maintenance is not generally a British priority. Like personnel (see Chapter 3) it suffers from the fact that it does not make anything, or sell anything, or even launder the money (it just spends some). Again people without experience of industry would be surprised how often machinery breaks down, with consequent disruption of work and schedules.

Finally in the technical connection there is the question of the technical education and virtuosity of the work force. It seems likely that there may be differences between countries in these respects. British managers who visit Japan, for example, frequently comment on the higher level of technical knowledge and skill displayed by Japanese workers. This contrast would hold for West Germany too where level for level the individual is likely to have more technical training: the graduate engineer in West Germany has had over five years at university, the non-graduate engineer (say the equivalent of the HNC engineer in Britain) has had three years' full-time training starting at the age of 18, the foreman is generally qualified, the skilled worker has completed a more demanding apprenticeship, the semi-skilled worker has often completed what is called a semi-apprenticeship, and so on. Particularly at the lower levels, the effect of all this is to produce a workforce which is more multi-competent, can do more things, is less likely to be held up waiting for someone else to come and do something (remember there is no demarcation problem either), and can handle technical contingencies better. This all makes a contribution to general efficiency and thus to delivery punctuality.

Industrial relations

In the introductory discussion of strikes in Chapter 4 we argued that, from the standpoint of any given manager, the likelihood of a strike in his own factory is not very high. This is quite true, but masks the effects of indirect strikes, which are often important in questions of delivery punctuality. In other words, a strike at the factory of a supplier, or a strike among delivery drivers, or industrial action somewhere in the power supply or transport or communications system, or even a strike at the premises of the customer which impedes the delivery of finished goods to him, are all more consequent for delivery performance and more probable. If one analyses particular cases of delivery failure, industrial action is quite likely to be a factor, but usually an 'off-stage' one.

At the next level down there is the whole gamut of industrial relations issues described and illustrated in the previous chapter which may have an incrementally disruptive effect on production, and which certainly engage the time and attention of those who organise production. What is more, whereas in Germany many of these industrial relations issues are by the nature of the system directed towards the personnel department, in Britain it is production managers and supervisors who tend to be in the front line.

The question of overtime, discussed in Chapter 4 as an example of a recurrent and contentious industrial relations issue, is again relevant to a consideration of the range of causes of delivery failure. The critical point is that although overtime would appear to be management's obvious recourse if things are running behind schedule, in practice overtime is a much less flexible instrument. It may be difficult to 'turn on' for a particular group, it is generally difficult to 'turn off', and if a company has been working (institutionalised) overtime for years anyway then there is no resource in reserve.

The paradox of finance

Although business firms exist to make a profit, some of the decisions to which their finance departments contribute actually make this rather less likely. Some of these contingencies have been hinted at already in the present chapter and include a reluctance to spend on plant and equipment renewal, and on maintenance. In discussing the purchasing function in Chapter 3 we also noted a tendency of finance managers to subordinate all considerations to that of 'cash now'.

With regard to the particular question of a company's delivery performance there are two other negative effects of financial considerations.

In many engineering companies which are handling a variety of jobs, these jobs have a price. What is more, knowledge of the price is not a unique privilege of higher management but in many cases something known to production managers, foremen and workers.

In such cases there is a well-known tendency for those allocating or picking jobs to give priority to ones with a high invoice value, especially if they are nice and straightforward. It simply sounds better to be able to say that already your section has turned out work worth £X,000 to the company, and it is only Thursday. This is fine for staking out profit in the early part of performance monitored time periods, but it may involve some distortion of the production schedule. Maybe the jobs that are needed first, are *promised* first to customers, are ones that are neither big nor straightforward, but have been in the queue a long time.

The second possible negative effect is a variation on the first. Performance by production entities is typically monitored by cash value over time periods. As with the price-labelling of individual jobs just discussed this is a totally rational state of affairs, and serves to remind people that the point of the operation is to make some money. But again, it may lead to distortion of the customer schedule. As the end of such accounting periods approach, and especially the end of the financial year, there is a strong tendency for production managers to pull forward Juicy Jobs (easy and lucrative) and push back less succulent morsels. But again this may lead to the completion in early April of jobs not promised until June but the further neglect of things the customer wanted in March.

Culture's consequence

There is a final, if nebulous, point to be made about the determinants of poor delivery performance. The whole sequence of events leading to the completion and delivery of an order on time involve many dependencies. In earlier chapters we have tended to highlight the dependencies internal to the company in the sense of relations between departments, and meetings as a means of co-ordination and problem solving. The consideration of factors relating to delivery performance, however, tends to draw attention to external dependencies especially with regard to suppliers. Now if we deliberately exaggerate to make the point, it is a situation where everyone's inefficiency contributes to everyone else's. The more delivery failure there is in the system, the more delivery failure there will be. The more industrial action, even in the public sector, the more disruption elsewhere. The less money spent on equipment renewal and maintenance, the more breakdowns and stoppages, the more aggro for workers whose piece-rate earnings are disrupted, the more industrial action, more lateness, more pressures and counter-pressures. Probably the most depressing part of the British performance in this context is the fact that the recession has not been accompanied by any obvious improvement in delivery performance, though by any rational and commercial criterion it should have been.

The delivery question in West Germany

Having gone a long way down the road of analysing what is generally viewed as a characteristic British failing, it is worth looking at the same phenomenon in West Germany for points of contrast. Perhaps one of the most widely held beliefs about Germans is that they care about time, punctuality and deadlines. It is a belief which is on the whole sustained by familiarity with industrial firms in that country. This value difference even comes out in the language.

In this discussion in English we have been using slightly contrived and infelicitous phrases like 'delivery performance' and 'delivery punctuality', which do not trip lightly off the layman's tongue. In German this little problem of self-expression would not arise. There is a word, *Termin*, which indicates deadline or due date, which is a standard expression, widely used and universally understood. The word is also redolent with serious-minded concern. What is more, there is an expression, *Termintreue*, which means literally deadline faithfulness, which expresses for Germans the idea of fulfilling delivery commitments with honour. This is also a standard expression, falling naturally from the lips of the German production controller. Indeed there are a whole range of *Termin*-based words, compound nouns and derived adjectives, which testify to the German concern.

Now it is fair to say that this concern with *Termintreue* is not in the literal sense of the phrase *'all* in the mind'. The first manifestation is that German managers give the attainment of *Termintreue* a higher priority, they demonstrably worry about it, and feel unmanned by any failure to achieve it. And the second manifestation is that they engage in action likely to make *Termintreue* a reality rather than an ideal. Much of this is in the form of common-sense planning and looking ahead. German managers do not like to be 'caught on the hop'. They are not keen on fire-fighting and crisis handling, less adept at devising instant expedients to cope with circumstantial difficulties than are their British colleagues, and less practised at this. So they tend to move forward in an orderly way, from one prepared position to another, with adequate supplies, time to spare, and something to fall back on. There is a lot of looking ahead, making sure the things that will be needed are going to be available, reminding people of their future commitments, and trying to anticipate difficulties.

The German attitude to procurement, the getting of materials and components, is an interesting case in point. As has been noted, there are both fewer strikes and fewer other industrial relations disruptions in Germany, the climate is more favourable generally, and supplier reliability is high. Notwithstanding all this, German companies are much more concerned to have alternative suppliers lined up and tuned in than are their British counterparts. German zeal for alternative sources is boundless, and this must be one contributory factor to the general state of affairs in which there are few shortages. Incidentally, it is perhaps indicative that in Britain we use an American expression, dual sourcing, to denote alternative suppliers, whereas the Germans use their own expression. The phrase is *zweites Bein*, literally second leg, to denote an alternative supplier. Though the characteristic German response to the question: do you have an alternative source of supply for . . .? is to say they have a fourth or fifth leg (the German company as procurement centipede).

There are one or two other things that German companies seem to do more than British ones which contribute to the good reputation for delivery punctuality. One might almost call them a part of German business policy, except that the phrase business policy is usually reserved for grander things than making customers happy with prompt deliveries.[6]

To start with there is the whole question of taking procurement seriously which we have just outlined. Second there is the related organisational point, broached in Chapter 1, that it is more common in German firms for the purchasing section to report to a production manager. This is not an unmitigated 'good thing', and in discussing the role of the purchasing department in Chapter 3 we put the full case for the purchasing function being independent. But the one thing that having purchasing under the control of production is good for, is getting supplies on time. A third consideration is that no company likes to have a lot of money tied up in stocks, either stocks of finished goods awaiting sale or distribution, or stocks of purchased materials and components needed for manufacture. Having said this, there are differences of degree, and our strong impression is that German companies work on more generous safety margins. In giving an example of the range of *ad hoc* meetings in Chapter 2 we cited a German maintenance manager who was worried in February about running out of central heating fuel in May. It may be an extreme case, but it does reflect a state of mind. What is more, even if this state of affairs is an accountant's nightmare it does ensure continuity of operations. The question is, should one pay the price? A fourth consideration is subcontracting. Our view is that German companies are more likely to use sub-contracting for straight capacity regulating purposes, to even out the high and low demands on the production capacity of the firm, than to use it for accounting, or even political reasons as in the example given in Chapter 4. Properly set up, a sub-contracting network is the best guarantee that there is against failure to finish orders on time.

Other factors relevant to German delivery performance have already been mentioned. The average age of factory buildings, plant and equipment is lower there than it is here. This is, of course, partly a result of the destruction inflicted on Germany in the Second World War, but this is not a complete explanation. It is not difficult these days to find German companies ensconced in their second or third new post-war premises. Maintenance is easier and, as suggested earlier, a higher priority (better funded). Expenditure on plant and machinery is considerable and that too is regarded as a pre-eminently just 'business expense'. The combined effect of these factors is ease of manufacturing operations, fewer breakdowns and disruptions.

But perhaps the ultimate explanation of the German performance lies in personality. A fascinating study of the work-related attitudes of employees of a multi-national company in several countries, including West Germany, has come up with the finding that the Germans in particular may be characterised as having a low tolerance for ambiguity.[7] It means in common language they are a bit insecure and neurotic. Now this low tolerance for ambiguity is highly relevant to planning for good delivery performance. This fear of the unknown (will it be on time, what can go wrong, will some problem that I have not even thought of crop up?) will lead to meticulous organisation, contingency plans, and always having something in reserve ('just in case!'). There is something to be said for insecurity.

Delivery performance and management in action

So far we have followed the intention declared at the outset of exploring two questions: what factors impede good delivery performance, and why do the Germans seem to do it better? This has been an analytical exercise rather than a (specialised) descriptive account of things that managers do. In the last couple of pages we will redress the balance a little, by taking up the question: what do managers actually do in connection with delivery performance?

Production managers and the organisation of delivery

Many of the relevant things have been implied already, or outlined in some other connection, so that this section is a matter of tying together loose ends.

First, as was shown in Chapter 2, production managers regularly attend and sometimes chair production progress or production control meetings (the *Termingespräch* in German firms) where the progress of various jobs and orders is reviewed, difficulties are highlighted, and counter-action devised. One of the most common bits of counter-action so devised is putting pressure on suppliers to speed up (or rectify things already sent) and production managers often do this themselves even if the purchasing function is not under their control. Second, there is corresponding action by production managers inside the firm typically in the form of badgering and leaning on other people to do things − pressing the goods inwards section to inspect and release supplies, and pressing final inspection to actually inspect, pressing design and engineering to produce drawings, specifications, parts-lists, tools and methods; maintenance for repairs; and the sales department for early warning.

Third, there is a miscellany of actions in which production managers engage that all contribute to delivery performance indirectly. The most obvious are responding to industrial relations issues and hopefully solving them long before they escalate into industrial action (especially in Britain) and concern with everything to do with the firm's productive apparatus in a technical sense. This last covers things like work on investment plans, capital expenditure budgets, the organisation of maintenance, planning or introduction of methods and layout changes, and so on.

Then there is another level of what might be called 'instant therapy' activity. This is in the form of interventionist moves to save or rectify jobs that have 'slipped' ('slippage' in Britain is the euphemism for running late; it is rather subtle in suggesting some geological movement beyond human control). Actions at this level include re-prioritising (changing the order so that the most critical job gets done on time); re-allocating critical jobs to fast workers or groups with a known high output; instituting overtime and shiftwork as solutions as was illustrated in the last chapter on industrial relations; and swopping jobs between machines or production lines – sometimes there are gains to be made by exchanges between NC and conventional machines.

Lastly, in this connection, production managers achieve something by maintaining a threatening presence, and spreading the impression that anyone who gets it wrong will get 'chewed out': some of the old-style German managers in the study showed themselves to be particularly good at this delegation of blame and chastisement of industrial sin. In one of the English companies the senior production manager spoke of going round the works giving everyone 'a little injection of nervous energy' to key them up for a taut performance on a critical order.

Top management and delivery performance

If one asks what in Britain is the involvement of higher management in the realisation of good delivery performance, the answer has to be, not a lot. In a way, this is as it should be. Top management has other things to worry about, and so long as the organisation of delivery performance is going well they may justifiably keep out of it. But the critical point is that in many companies in Britain it is patently not going well, and this must be seen as an indictment of higher management.

There is another way of looking at it. In a certain sense probing this question by means of an Anglo-German comparison is misleading. The German half of the equation is fine – a neurotic disposition to take it seriously and get it right. But what about Britain? It is not some happy-go-lucky, *mañana*-oriented backwater, where lovable locals lounge in the sunshine, sipping nectar: it is a sober, industrial country in north-west Europe which in fact produced the world's first industrial revolution. It is not that British companies do not care about delivery punctuality. It is rather that they do not care enough to pay the price, or that they put other things first. Spending money, especially on equipment renewal, would help to raise the national performance in this respect, but in our view money is not the most important input. Above all it requires an input of organisational energy and imagination, operating at the level of the preventive and systematic, not at that of the issues raised in this chapter. Only policy devised at the top will resolve problems of a recurrent and entirely predictable nature.

Summary

This chapter has addressed the questions: what are the obstacles to delivery punctuality, and how do the Germans manage to do better? To set the scene, international comparative evidence and local British data were cited to signify the extent of the problem. Examples to show the complexity of such issues were also introduced. The discussion of obstacles to good delivery performance included a consideration of the procurement operation, the role of the quality control department, the effects of a relatively ageing technical apparatus, maintenance provision, shortcomings in design and engineering, the effects of industrial action and especially the indirect effects, and the inhibiting effect of some financial practices. In the corresponding, though briefer, examination of these issues in West Germany we noted a higher level of spending on plant and equipment, more emphasis on the technical aspects of production, and the apparent prevalence of certain business policy moves conducive to good delivery performance.

Finally we sought to indicate the practical involvement of production managers in the question of good delivery performance, and drew attention to the culpable neglect of its importance by the higher management of many companies in Britain.

Notes

1 The relative performance of several European countries on the question of delivery is shown in Peter W. Turnbull and Malcolm T. Cunningham (eds), *International Marketing and Purchasing*, Macmillan, 1981.
2 Data illustrating the poor performance of some British companies is given in C.C. New, *Managing Manufacturing Operations*, British Institute of Management, 1976.

3 Ibid.
4 Ibid.
5 Poor delivery performance is also suggested in C.C. New and M.T. Sweeney, 'Throughput Efficiency and Delivery Performance in the UK Mechanical Engineering Industry: A Report Detailing the Analysis and Results of the Study performed in a Collaborating Firm', Cranfield Institute of Technology, November 1980.
6 This idea of a German business policy oriented to achieving good delivery performance is developed in Peter Lawrence, 'National Culture and Business Policy', *Journal of General Management*, Spring 1983.
7 For a fascinating study of different attitudes to work in a variety of countries see Geert Hofstede, *Culture's Consequences. International Differences in Work Related Values*, Sage Publications, Beverly Hills and London, 1980.

Further reading

PETER W. TURNBULL and MALCOLM T. CUNNINGHAM (eds), *International Marketing and Purchasing*, Macmillan, 1981, is an excellent, research-based survey of the issues pertaining to successful exporting, including delivery punctuality.

C.C. NEW, *Managing Manufacturing Operations*, British Institute of Management, 1976, is good for giving some bare facts about delivery performance in Britain while looking at the broader context of manufacturing.

S.P. HUTTON and P.A. LAWRENCE, 'Production Management and Training', Report to the Science and Engineering Research Council, 1980 (also available from the University of Loughborough library) contains a neat itemisation of impediments to good delivery performance.

S. CAULKIN, 'Delivering the Goods', *Management Today*, January 1976.

A. CHATTERTON and T. ROWAN, 'How to Deliver', *Management Today*, May 1977.

D. CORKE, 'Late Deliveries? Today there is no Excuse', *The Production Engineer*, June 1977.

S. PAULDEN, *How to Deliver on Time*, Gower, 1977.

S. PAULDEN, 'How Salesmen Make Orders Overdue', *Marketing*, November 1977.

Discussion questions

1 'Delivery failure is caused by strikes.' Discuss.
2 What may a company do to minimise the likelihood of being let down by suppliers?
3 What are the critical interfaces in a company for the organisation of good delivery?
4 Who ought to set delivery dates?
5 How is the superior German performance to be explained?
6 Devise *a business policy* to ensure a good delivery record.

6

Decisions and problems

There is a broad distinction between policy decisions and problem solving decisions, and this short chapter is about the latter. Policy decisions relate to the overall objectives of a company and strategies for their achievement. Although these are the sort of decisions that managers are seen as taking in the popular imagination, such decisions are in fact few and far between and concentrated in the upper echelons. There is, however, no shortage of problems and problem solving decisions, and that holds for all levels including the senior ones.

The distinction between the two types of decision is not watertight. A policy decision may solve problems. Suppose, for example, that top management rules that potential American buyers shall be given any modifications to the standard products that they request, however complicated, to help the company become established in the American market; this would be a policy decision that would also in a sense solve the problem of disagreements between sales and production on this issue (see Chapter 3 for a full analysis of disagreements between sales and production). And the reverse can occur, where a problem solving decision is made which has policy implications. Imagine, for instance, a production manager frustrated by the arrival of defective components from a sole supplier: he might respond by asking the purchasing department to identify a new supplier for this item, and a second supplier for all components currently obtained from a single source.

Notwithstanding this two-way qualification, the majority of decisions are simply problem solving decisions. Furthermore, although many of them might in principle have policy implications, few have them in fact. So the intention here is to present a sample of the problems and the kinds of decision they invoke.

In two senses there has already been some treatment of the problems-decisions theme. Many of these problems are actually formulated and articulated in management meetings, and the same meeting often decides on a course of action. So in the discussion and illustration of the range of meetings which managers attend given in Chapter 2 we have already shown a lot of such problem issues coming to light and in some cases have indicated the decision-action on them. The second sense is that later chapters dealing with particular issues — interdepartmental relations, industrial relations, delivery performance — have also by definition been oriented to practical problems and have been replete with real examples. None the less we would like to enlarge the field by offering a few single company based problem samples, while deliberately omitting industrial relations issues which have been well covered already.

On the basis of even a few company examples readers will probably discern two trends. First, there is a lot of patterning, from company to company, even country to country, where the same sort of issues recur, or at least issues which could be listed under the same thematic heading. But second, and paradoxically, there are often one or two odd-ball issues as well, things that are particular to a given industry, or peculiar to the situation of the manager as an individual. Consider as a first example a marine equipment company in the Midlands, employing some 1,000 people on site. This is the series of problem issues confronted by the works director in the two day period of the study.

Marine Equipment Company

This company, part of a larger group, is technically up-market with a quality reputation to maintain. What is more, some of its sales are to government bodies who impose high standards controlled by their own inspectors. This is relevant to some of the issues encountered:

1 The company was about to host a conference-cum-visit of all the managing directors of the works in the group, a visit which would include a tour of the works themselves. This posed for the works director the question of making sure everything was shipshape for the tour. Accordingly he instructed the foremen to enforce strictly the teabreak times on the day concerned, and to make sure the NC machines were running during the tour. He agreed with the sales manager to cover up a machine returned by an overseas customer for modifications, and arranged to have dirty lorries washed. The tour went off without a hitch.

2 The company was experiencing considerable difficulty in obtaining castings (see Chapter 5 on the general problem of castings and its knock-on effect for delivery performance) to the right specification, the foundry which was the main supplier of castings proving inadequate. In the course

of the two days the works director had discussions with a quality control manager about whether some of the castings recently supplied by this foundry were acceptable or not; with his subordinate purchasing manager on the results of the latter's trouble-shooting visit to the foundry (who were sorry but admitted they did not really know what to do to get them right); the works director discussed with the same purchasing manager the search for alternative suppliers (the purchasing manager had already identified one and made a preliminary visit); and with engineers he discussed the flexibility of these technical specifications with reference to a possible new supplier using a different manufacturing method.

3 The representative of an important customer company informed the works director that metal swarf had been discovered in a pipe in a piece of equipment supplied by the company. This swarf does not in fact cause any danger or malfunction; it simply suggests carelessness. The works director responded by conducting a witch-hunt with his production superintendents on how it happened and how it is to be prevented in the future.

4 The company was having difficulty in getting materials from particular suppliers. The works director investigated, and discovered that these suppliers were holding back because they had not been paid for earlier consignments. He then put pressure on the finance department to have them paid quickly.

5 A two-dimensional bottleneck in goods inwards inspection came to light where the customer's inspector and the works own inspector spend so long ruling on items bought-in from suppliers that it was frustrating the manufacturing programme. No solution emerged; it was rather a question of a problem to be lived with.

6 One of this manager's superintendents complained that tradesmen were being traded between maintenance and production by means of informal agreements at foreman level. A maintenance foreman, for example, would 'borrow' a couple of welders from production to do a particular job and just fix it with the relevant production foreman. The superintendent asked to have this informal trading stopped, and the works director agreed.

7 A particularly prickly human problem arose in the form of a young employee who had just finished a welding apprenticeship, but the company had no work for him. To let this young employee look for a job elsewhere would appear particularly bad since he had won a national level award for the quality of his apprentice welding work. This difficulty was compounded by the fact that he had no other obvious abilities and was therefore difficult to deploy in some other area of work. No decision was taken, beyond consulting relevant supervisors.

Note the untidy nature of decision-making in industry. Some of the problems are pervasive rather than tangible and isolated, and as with industrial relations problems (Chapter 4) some are 'solved' by postponement, resignation, or after-the-event response.

Now let us consider an entirely different industry in West Germany.

A German brewery

This brewery in Bavaria is an interesting case in that there are two factors which push up the incidence of problems requiring some decision, although again in some cases these problems are ongoing rather than isolated at a point in time. The first is the fact that this brewery, formerly independent, had been taken over by a large semi-conglomerate: takeovers lead to tension and change. The second is that the manager himself was relatively new at the time of the study having been in post for less than eleven months: he was an outsider, not an internal promotee, who had been invited to apply. He clearly represents the force for rationality and change implied by the new ownership. The brewery employs some 1,200 people on site, and the manager is two levels above the foreman reporting to the technical director.

1 There was for this manager an ongoing problem deriving from the fact that he was a recent outside appointment for a post for which there had been several internal candidates, including one of his direct subordinates. There were clearly difficulties with this particular subordinate, although the manager described the situation as improving.

2 There was a technical filtering problem which was being handled by an outside consultant, though at the time of the study no solution had been reached. The consultant observed to the manager: 'You think you've got problems; you should see them in Stuttgart!'

3 Some glass splinters were found in a storage tank, and the manager reprimanded the foreman concerned; when the latter began to offer excuses he was given a second reprimand to the effect that 'that's how the English disease starts.'

4 It was recognised at one of the scheduled recurrent meetings that the interface between production and distribution was unsatisfactory. The manager required one of his subordinates to produce a production plan that would be more meaningful to distribution and allow them to organise their work better.

5 The study took place during the winter in the middle of a flu epidemic, so that the company had hired some temporary workers to

replace those off sick. At the manager's weekly meeting with his foremen the latter raised complaints about these temporary workers, the worst indictment being that some group had been caught swilling beer produced by a rival brewery. The manager urged closer supervision and forbade the deployment of these unsatisfactory temporary workers in an upstairs area where they could keep a crate of beer under the table.

6 There was a technical difficulty with putting the caps on bottles which also had a gold foil cover; it was feared that the caps were not going on tight enough. After discussion at the foreman meeting the manager passed the issue to the quality control department for further investigation.

7 The company sales forecast suggested lower sales than in the previous year, and there was a general purge on costs which manifested itself in several ways. At the foreman meeting, for example, the manager announced that the use of steam was excessive and urged the foremen to effect a reduction.

8 Top management was contemplating some internal reorganisation, and two young PhDs were working on a revised organisation structure. The parts of the plan which affected our manager were:

(a) raising the maintenance and quality control managers to the same level as the production manager: they all reported to the same boss (the technical director) but maintenance and quality control were understood to be junior (and did not have a company 220 Mercedes);

(b) adding an EDP (electronic data processing) manager at the same level; the company had computer process control installed under the supervision of the production manager who had made himself an expert on this, and published technical articles on it;

(c) putting in an extra rank between all these people and the technical director, to reduce the latter's span of control.

The position of the production manager was somewhat ambiguous. On the one hand he was identified with the new, rational reforming management, and saw that he could serve as a bridge between the old hands and the young graduates; on the other, some of the proposed changes were not really in his interest, especially the insertion of an extra (higher) rank in the hierarchy. No final decisions were taken, but the production manager had a running dialogue with the two corporate planners, alternately offering moral support and playing devil's advocate.

9 The production manager and one of his subordinates planned to make a *Studienreise* (study trip) abroad. They had a meeting and decided what breweries and other establishments they wanted to visit. This 'academicising' of work in industry is very German.

10 The sales forecast suggested a 6 per cent shortfall on the sales of the previous year which led to a critical meeting between the finance department and various people from production. At this meeting the production director agreed to various cost-cutting measures, including a reduction of overtime working, and enforced them on his subordinate managers.

11 The admin section produced a print-out of telephone charges by individual user; the print-out listed all the dialled destinations as well. The manager was so incensed at these rising costs that he reprimanded various colleagues and subordinates (and congratulated one or two whose telephone costs were less than in the corresponding period in the previous year), had the switchboard block all the calls from one subordinate until further notice, and instituted inquiries about another who had been calling an unknown number in Lyons, France, with suspicious frequency. Rank for rank, German managers are more likely to get involved in details than their English colleagues, especially technical details. A further small example occurred when the production manager inspected the fermentation section: here he told off the superintendent because the lampshade in the lift was dirty!

12 Finally during the same tour of the fermentation section the manager checked the checks that the quality control section should be making, and found some derelictions. This led to a confrontation with the quality control boss as a result of which more rigorous controls and a new reporting procedure were agreed.

For the reasons given at the outset this manager was in a particularly interesting position. When invited to look back over the eleven months he had served with this company he saw his most important decisions as:

1 Sacking a foreman for incompetence; this in Germany is about the equivalent of sacking a high court judge in Britain.

2 Putting in a computer to control the brewing process.

3 Instituting a proper budgetary control system.

4 Replacing various items of old equipment.

The technical emphasis in these is very German.

As a last example let us consider a much smaller company, one making a range of agro-engineering products in the north of England.

English agro-engineering company

This company has some 400 employees on site, though it is part of a larger group. Its work is to some extent seasonal, and the study took place in the slack season with a low level of orders, no overtime working, and some cancellations. The manager concerned is the manufacturing director, two levels above the foreman rank.

1 First he interviewed, and decided to reject, an applicant for the post of production superintendent, to replace a long-serving colleague about to retire. This episode is of more than passing interest, in that when it comes to production management posts, especially the lower level ones, many companies tend to 'grow their own timber'. When an internal candidate is not to hand, as in this case, they are often rather faltering in their efforts to find a candidate on the open market. Part of the problem is that they are not used to it, and in part they have difficulty specifying the job requirements. They end up looking for someone who is 'just like Frank' (or whoever it is who is leaving), right down to wearing horn rim glasses and growing roses in his spare time.

2 The company has a temporary cash flow problem. One of the things the manufacturing director does in response to this is to go through a list of purchase orders for components, and also for extras to go with the company's products in order to make up an ensemble for the customer, and axe those that are not urgent.

3 Many machining jobs involve a getting ready/setting up operation before the machining starts. Under a piece-work system some allowance is made for this setting up time, so the actual amount of time taken and/or allowed is of some significance. In this company setting up time had been a matter of foreman's discretion, and the whole thing had been kept in check by a particularly strict foreman. But after the departure of this individual setting up times had got out of hand and were a force for wage drift. The manufacturing director recognised this and directed his production engineer to do realistic timings to regularise it all.

4 The company were about to begin the manufacture of their biggest and best products in the USA to make an impact on the American market. The manufacturing director decided to send his production engineer out to oversee some of the technical-organisational aspects of this operation: it included the need to demetricate the technical specifications (we may have joined the Common Market but the USA has not) and to organise a net of suppliers and sub-contractors able to work to UK norms.

5 A shortage of electric motors to be fitted to the company's products is recognised, and the manufacturing director authorised a search for alternative suppliers.

6 The manager presses the finance department to pay a major German supplier who is threatening to cut off supplies.

7 At the weekly production control meeting it emerges that a Swedish

customer has failed to respond to telexes asking for an elaboration of the customer's requirements; this prevents the job being completed on time. It comes to light that the Swedish buyer is only a middleman who is probably on-selling into eastern Europe, which no doubt explains the delay.

8 The manufacturing director agrees to investigate a case where supplies have been requisitioned by the inventory controller but not in fact ordered.

9 At the production control meeting they discuss a case where a customer in Ireland has requested that the completion date for a job be brought forward by two weeks: they decide to say no since the customer has failed to make drawings for requested modifications available.

10 After a discussion with his production controller the manufacturing director decides to sanction various initiatives in the controller's section including:

    (a) reshuffling personnel because a foreman is leaving;

    (b) reducing a senior foreman to the ranks for incompetence;

    (c) investigating a worker with a record of bad time keeping.

11 The manufacturing director decided to forbid the departure of a lorry to Iraq with a consignment of machinery because no proper letter of credit had been received from the customer (i.e. a document which would guarantee payment by the customer or someone on his behalf which could not be revoked).

12 The last of the confronted problems is particularly sad, and something of a sign of the times. The company had been doing good business in the Middle East, making most deliveries by road, using a local haulier. The latter called to say he was currently owed £60,000 and demanded half straightaway to satisfy his own creditors. The company could not pay without borrowing from the group, which was embarrassing because they had already had to do so.

General points

If we return to the two considerations urged at the outset, it will be clear that there is both a patterning of problems and decision-issues, and some idiosyncratic cases. To take the first point, things to do with supplies — getting them on time, getting them right, getting them paid for, finding alternatives — keep on cropping up. Quality issues are recurrent — incoming and outgoing, responding to customer complaints, bringing in consultants to solve particular problems, relations between production and quality control. And then costs and cash flow questions arise repeatedly — cuttings costs, reducing overtime, saving fuel, cutting telephone bills, postponing non-immediate purchases, and so on.

At the same time there are idiosyncratic issues: what to do with an unemployable boy-wonder welder, how to cope with an Irish customer who wants it earlier than agreed but has not told you what it is. Or there are some entirely non-routine decisions including computer installation and opening a manufacturing subsidiary in the USA.

We suggested at the beginning that the outsider's view of management problems and decision making is probably too august, centring on brow-furrowed executives wrestling with multi-million investment decisions, whereas in practice a lot of it is much more homely than this as we have shown. There is another misapprehension which is to assume that the problems and decisions are all legitimate production-sales-business related issues. Again, as we have shown, many of them are but it is not at all unusual for some non-business occurrence to have all sorts of problem-decision implications for the company concerned. We will round off this consideration of problem solving decisions by offering an example from a company in each of the countries, starting with Britain.

When the works blows up

One of the studies at a company in the Midlands making light commercial vehicles took place a few days after a gas main explosion had demolished the dispatch building. This involved a whole sequence of problems and decisions for the management.

First, they had to construct a temporary dispatch building, in the middle of winter, with no notice. This in turn led to a conflict between the manager in charge of dispatch and the site engineers as to the level of facilities that was possible and the exact siting of the building. Second, the disruption of the dispatch operation meant that there was an excessive number of completed vans waiting to be shipped out. Normally there would be about 240 completed vehicles, but at the height of the crisis the number reached 2,554. A lot of space is needed to store 2,500 vans. The dispatch of completed vehicles question in turn involved special measures including bringing in foremen on overtime pay at the weekend to act as traffic cops and prevent wild driving around the works.

Third, there was a general manpower shortage. For the time of year the company reckoned on 9 per cent absenteeism, and in fact had only 7 per cent, but with the manufacturing backlog caused by the explosion there were not enough workers. The company responded with a complicated overtime and supervision plan. The explosion and its aftermath threw up so many working problems that the managing director ran a 'crisis meeting' first thing each morning to try to work out solutions.

Cut off from the world

We referred earlier to one of the studies at a German company located in a town cut off from the rest of the world by a blizzard. Again the point is that the precipitating factor, the weather, has nothing to do with business operations conceived in either technical or commercial terms, yet for several days it had a marked impact on the company concerned.

First came the critical decision on whether or not to carry on work. After sending workers home on the afternoon of the first day when the local radio station announced the impending closure of many roads out of town the company in fact mounted a very successful 'business as usual' campaign for the rest of the week, even having a late shift working in the machine shop. This in turn required various subsidiary arrangements, mentioned in Chapter 2 in the context of illustrating the range of *ad hoc* discussions – organising homeward transport, offering to pay taxi fares for late shift workers, executives booking into hotel rooms in town, and so on.

Second, there was an element of executive musical chairs with things being decided and done by those managers actually present with a high level of managerial absenteeism. This gave almost emergency powers to the production manager who lived locally but whose boss was unable to reach the works after the first day.

Third, there were all sorts of practical measures simply to keep the works functioning, involving close liaison between the production and maintenance managers. The company had its own snow plough, and managed to acquire another; it also improvised snow ploughs by mounting pieces of curved metal on the front of fork lift trucks. With this equipment, and by throwing in snow-clearing teams starting each morning at 5 a.m., they managed to keep the factory and access roads open, and the car parks clear. Getting indoors piles of components stacked outside before they became buried in the snow was another emergency measure.

Finally we have already referred to the incident of a transformer breakdown using it as an illustration of the spectacular quiescence of German workers. This incident had another effect, namely that of enabling the production manager to get a new factory roof on the current capital expenditure budget. Here we have the ultimate link between snow-balls and business policy.

Decision making and perfect knowledge

A final issue that should be raised here concerns the relationship between information and decision making. It is clearly highly desirable that those who take decisions in industry should be equipped with all the relevant information so that the decision may be both more meaningful and more rational. The simple point we would like to make is that this is often impossible or impracticable.

This simple point is worth making because a major strand in post-war management literature has been concerned with the rationality and optimisation of decision processes. This trend has been given a further thrust in the last twenty years with the development first of main frame computers, then of minis and micros, the rise of management service departments, and the elaboration of management information systems and the forward march of information technology. All this is clearly helpful to the manager. The danger lies in the belief that perfect information always can and will be available.

For many of the management problems identified in this book the formal processes referred to in the previous paragraph are relevant. At the same time there are limitations. Some of these problems cannot await the assembling of relevant information before a decision is made. In other cases a quasi-intuitive judgment of people is involved. Or the decision does not really depend on information gathering at all but is a question of politics and negotiation. In yet other cases there are so many variables that there is no way of holding some constant while playing with others. These remarks are not meant as a plea for a return to a pre-computer executive dark age. The point is rather that information technology must be the manager's servant, not the agency of his emasculation.

Summary

We began by distinguishing between policy making and problem solving decisions and, while noting that the distinction is not absolute, indicated a concentration on problem solving decisions. To this end we examined a variety of problems and the ensuing decisions of managers at three companies in the study. This exercise, as well as the examples of topics dealt with at various kinds of meeting given in Chapter 2, make it clear that there is a certain patterning in the form of recurrent issues — procurement, quality, costs and cash flow, scheduling questions and, in Britain, industrial relations issues. At the same time there is a sprinkling of idiosyncratic issues requiring decisions, and a leaven of non-routine problems.

Having made the point that most managerial problem solving and decision making is rather less august than outsiders imagine, we argued that some of the impetus to problem solving decisions comes from events which have no connection at all with the nature of the business itself, and illustrated this proposition. Finally we suggested that the growing development of formal information systems and aids to managerial decision making should not deflect from a recognition that on many occasions the manager has to decide fast and without the benefit of all the relevant information.

Further reading

For the classic work in the formal decision making approach Herbert A. Simon, *Administrative Behaviour*, Collier-Macmillan Canada, 2nd edition, 1947.

P.A. LAWRENCE and R.A. LEE, *Insight into Management*, Oxford University Press, 1984, contains a chapter on operating problems and decisions in several functional areas.

Two books offering a more zesty approach to management decision making are:
ROBERT TOWNSEND, *Up the Organisation*, Michael Joseph, 1970.
ROBERT HELLER, *The Naked Manager*, Barrie & Jenkins, 1974.

Discussion questions

1 What is the feasibility and utility of the conventional distinction between policy decisions and problem-solving decisions?
2 What would you see as the likely problems of a company that has been taken over?
3 Take any of the company examples in the foregoing chapter and suggest policy decisions which would prevent the emergence of such problems.
4 How would you seek to overcome a middle-term problem of poor quality in a manufacturing company?

7

Life at the top

The purpose in the present chapter is to look at the work and distinctive responsibilities of higher level managers. It is a companion piece to the last chapter, but it is more open-ended, focusing on the distinctive concerns and experiences of higher managers rather than on tangibly identifiable problems and decisions. It is also more open-ended in drawing on a variety of contacts with top managers, not only on the Anglo-German study which has provided most of the material discussed so far, and using knowledge and experience of other countries as well as Britain and Germany. We are also operating a kind of hierarchical sliding scale by using a nice woolly concept like 'high level managers'. This means in fact starting with chief executives of major companies or heads of substantial operating divisions, working through general managers in charge of manufacturing establishments, and going on to higher production managers. So this is a less precise, but more imaginative exercise than that pursued in the last chapter.

Acquisitions

We will start with something exotic as well as dynamic. Acquiring other companies is a legitimate, if highly intermittent, concern of top managers. Broadly speaking there are two kinds of acquisition: strategic and opportunistic. Strategic acquisition is where the company bought has an operational significance for the buying company. The most likely form of this strategic acquisition is buying supplier companies so that the buyer gains control of its sources of raw materials, components, or sub-assemblies. This is known as vertical integration. More precisely one might call this vertical integration backwards, in that the company doing the acquisition gains control of a logically prior operation, getting hold of the things it needs to carry out its own manufacturing programme. But there is also vertical integration forwards where the buying company seeks to acquire companies which handle the produce at a post-manufacturing stage, for example, by buying a transport fleet, shipping line, a chain of distributors, or even an advertising agency. A company that managed to do both these things might achieve a very high level of vertical integration, having at the end of the day its own raw material sources, sub-contractors, transport, sales outlets and promotional advertising support.

To this hard version of vertical integration we might add the notion of what one writer has called quasi-vertical integration, where a big and powerful company comes to enjoy the fruits of ownership without actually owning these other (smaller) companies which are drawn into its net.[1] Consider in this connection a large retail organisation selling a miscellany of product ranges, some of these products being manufactured entirely by sub-contracting firms. If the retail organisation is sufficiently powerful it may achieve a high dominance over the sub-contractors, taking all their output, setting the prices very much in its own favour, laying down the product specifications, imposing its own quality standards, and determining what is called the call-off rate. The call-off is the number of items taken by the retail organisation per time period: it will be set at what the buyer initially thinks will be the right level, but then adjusted upwards and downwards to suit the buyer's convenience, with the supplier being left to handle these fluctuating demands on its productive capacity as best as it can. Such a situation of quasi-vertical integration may give the big buyer all the advantages of actual ownership (of the supplier) without its risks and liabilities.

So much for strategic acquisition. It is not in the context of the early 1980s wildly popular given the high cost of capital, general pessimism about growth and markets, and tendency of many companies to 'dig in' by concentrating on their core business while divesting themselves of the overhead costs of ancillary operations.

Opportunistic acquisitions are just what the term suggests: attempts to buy other companies simply because they are making money, or better still, buying other companies which may be made to make money by post-acquisition re-structuring. Or as one top manager we interviewed put it, opportunistic acquisition is all about 'going shopping for fat pigs'.

It is not an obvious point, but a recessionary climate tends to favour opportunistic acquisition. However stagnant the world economy, some companies somewhere have the capacity to make money, and the important thing is to grab them. One of the managers we interviewed is head of a holding company devoted entirely to acquiring and running such opportunistically acquired companies, the people reporting to him being all heads of recently acquired enterprises. This operation proceeds in a surprisingly inspirational way, with relatively little reliance on market analysis and growth forecasts. It is rather a matter of having business instincts crossed with a plenitude of contacts. So that the ideal acquisition is a company which is not actually doing marvellously well at the time of purchase, but one that can be made to perform, above all by picking the right person to run it, and then closely monitoring performance in financial terms.

Succession

The head of a company is by definition such an august personage that there is a natural tendency to think that he or she has always been there. Not so. All heads succeeded, or in some cases acceded, at a point in time. So that the traumas of succession may be an important part of the top management experience. And to bring together the theme of succession with the idea of acquisition, these traumas are likely to be particularly acute in the case of the acceding head of an acquired company.

Another of the top managers we interviewed had been in precisely this position at the start of his reign. He became head of a company abroad, newly acquired by his British-based multi-national. The acquisition was entirely rational, and eventually successful. The acquired company was an established family firm in another country, with good products and a good reputation for product quality. It gave the acquiring multi-national a manufacturing base in a new territorial area, and opened up wider market possibilities, since the multi-national could sell in this new area not only the produce of the acquired company but complementary products produced in the home factories. But this is only part of the story.

The newly acquired company had been neglected somewhat by the local owning family. Its profitability was not particularly good, financial controls were primitive, marketing unimaginative, and it was burdened with a lot of managerial deadwood – older managers lacking wider experience and poorly qualified in a formal sense. So that the post-succession phase was a 'valiant years' period marked by a struggle to establish personal credibility, financial restructuring, exploiting the marketing possibilities and building up a committed team of younger graduate managers.

Building up the business

When the economic climate is unfavourable there is a tendency to view success negatively. In such circumstances the good chief executive is one who manages to hold on to what the company already has, who preserves its profit margins and market share, perhaps in a situation of world wide over-capacity and declining overall market. But this is not enough. Companies survive by going forward, not standing still.

An example is offered by another of the managers we interviewed, the president of a company originally set up simply to make identification cards for banks and the post office in its home country. The company head, however, was unwilling to occupy this docile supplier role, and seized the opportunity to market exactly the same product-service to banks in other countries. He also spored an R & D operation which put the company ahead in the production of non-forgeable identity and access documentation so that it became an important manufacturer of credit cards, supplier of passports to other state governments and a pioneer in access control cards.

New applications

A variation on this theme of building up the business is the identification of new applications for products or services the company already provides. As one company president dryly put it, 'It is a whole lot easier to think of new applications for the things you already do than to conceive, design, and develop new products for an uncertain market.' An interview with the head of a telecommunications firm, an intensely competitive industry anyway, who suffered from the further disadvantage of being overshadowed by a larger telecommunications firm in the home country, offers an example. One of several new applications this manager described was an adaptation of their competence to provide an interference-proof radio telephone system which could be sold to foreign governments as a means of communicating with their extra-territorial embassies world-wide.

Analysis and turn round

Some top managers responsible for a large company or an important operating division emphasise analytical ability in accounts of their work, and in particular as the quality necessary to work out what to do to 'turn round' a company with falling profitability. It may not be obvious to outsiders just how complicated is the structure of the business that the man at the top has to have a view of, and therefore of the role of analysis. Consider as an example a manager in charge of a complete 'business area' of a major multi-national company. The business area is broken down into several divisions by product or product range. Each of these divisions is in turn made up of a variety of manufacturing works and R & D establishments in several countries. The business area is also divided up into twenty sales organisations, but the sales organisations cut across the seven product divisions. These sales organisations, that is to say, have a geographic basis, but any given sales organisation is responsible for the sale of products from all seven divisions in its area. Thus this business area has a matrix organisation as shown in Figure 7.1.

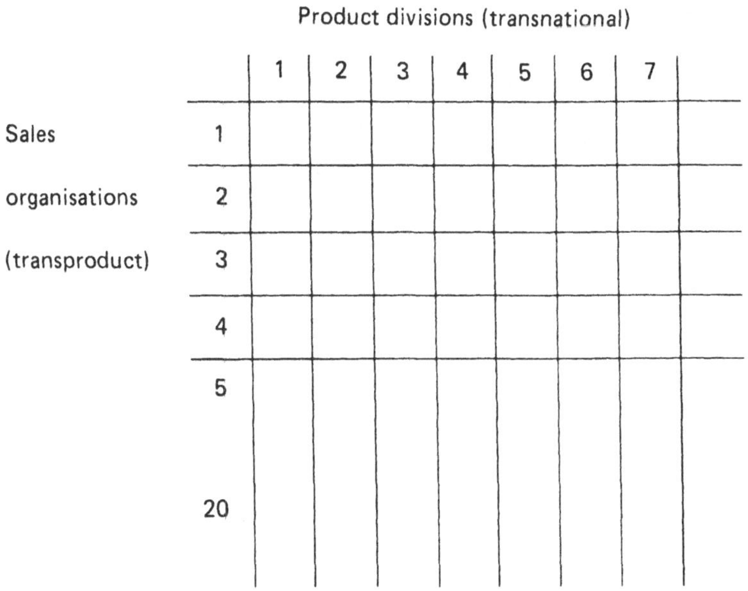

Product divisions (transnational)

		1	2	3	4	5	6	7	
Sales	1								
organisations	2								
(transproduct)	3								
	4								
	5								
	20								

Figure 7.1

So for a start the business area manager has twenty-seven immediate subordinates in the form of seven heads of product divisions and twenty heads of sales organisations, and these subordinates are spread around the world in every continent except Antarctica. Not only is twenty-seven a high span of control for a chief executive (many foremen have fewer subordinates than this) but the possibilities for disagreement among the subordinates are unlimited. Just imagine the head of the sales organisation in Canada claiming a declining demand for the produce of Division Three, whose manufacturing facility in Ontario ought therefore to be run down. Or the head of Division Five claiming that the reason they are doing little business in Western Europe in contrast to North America lies with the torpor and ineptitude of the heads of the sales organisations in Europe.

At the time this particular business area manager had taken over, his part of the company had been faced with falling profitability. He described four strategies for effecting a turn-round, which had been largely successful:

1 Pruning and closing unprofitable and apparently hopeless parts of the business. The manager volunteered that this is the easy part: any fool can close loss-making plants, but this does not necessarily give you a profit on what remains.

2 Having regular periodic discussions with groups of subordinates in which targets would be set and progress towards them reviewed at the next meeting. It is not an original idea, but it is acknowledged to be a powerful motivator. How can a manager not strive to fulfil an objective he has defined as viable in front of a group of his peers.

3 Starting some new R & D based business ventures, which would take a long time to pay off, so the sooner you start them the better.

4 Picking (better) people to do things: he had in fact replaced several of the division and sales organisation heads (see Figure 7.1).

In discussing the task of this business area manager we have chosen deliberately an example of a complicated business structure which puts a premium on analytical grasp. The important general point is that there will always be some demands for these abilities in a top manager. This particular manager summed it up by saying: 'You have to have the power of analysis to see what has to be done, and then you have to pick people to do it.'

Another point of interest in this manager's account concerns the criterion for 'picking people'. They are picked on the basis of track record, but in a very positive sense. Not only is it important for the 'pickable' subordinate to have increased profits and developed the business, but this has to have been done without relying exclusively on pruning and closures, and without leaving the organisation in a mess (anyone can make a profit for two years if they don't have to worry about what happens next).

Before we leave the example of this multi-national manager it should be said that his account of his work brings out another general aspect of the chief executive role. He claimed to spend over half the year away from head office, which meant in effect spending half the year abroad. Part of this time is obviously spent with immediate subordinates, but this manager emphasised that much of this away-from-base time was spent meeting customers. The general point at issue is that top managers often are drawn into sales. There is a real contrast here, because the same top manager will never be *directly* involved in production or engineering or R & D, even if he takes an interest in them and initiates changes in these areas, but he does on occasion act as salesman. If the customer is big and important enough he deals with the head of the company.

People and industrial relations

Top managers in Britain in particular emphasise some of the people related aspects of their work. In the survey by Charles Margerison referred to in Chapter 3 a sample of chief executives in Britain were asked to say why they thought they had been so successful and reached the top.[2] In the 'top twenty' explanations offered, people-related answers figured rather prominently, with reference to social skills and social ease, being able to get on with or relate to a wide variety of people, and being able to do deals with different people.

These findings accord with the author's experience in interviewing top managers in Britain. They not only display such social skills but are conscious of them and of their value.

Another particularly British feature is the role of the chief executive as industrial relations watch dog. He does not wish to be involved in the minutiae of industrial relations, but often maintains a watching brief, intervening to stop any one else inappropriately adopting confrontationist or adversarial tactics, or pursuing some objective blind to its consequences for industrial relations. The reverse is also true, though less frequently, in that an initiative likely to have adverse consequences for industrial relations will be cleared by the chief executive at the outset. In one of the British companies, for example, the production director, when faced with poor company performance, embarked on a multi-lateral programme to raise productivity. Many parts of this programme were in a sense a challenge to trade union power – ending overtime working and introducing shift work, obliging operators to do preventive maintenance, setting and adjusting; reducing seven maintenance trades to three; and making pay rises entirely conditional on gains in productivity.

Several times in this chapter reference has been made to the importance of judging and picking people – as successors, to replace deadwood, as people who can achieve the results required. There is a broader aspect to this as well. Chief executives have a more general responsibility for management development, that is, for training, developing, counselling and generally 'bringing on' their subordinate managers, and this responsibility goes beyond simply picking people for particular assignments.

Indeed in describing management development as a chief executive responsibility we are expressing it too narrowly. In discussing the work of personnel departments in Chapter 3 we argued that, especially in British companies, personnel managers may see themselves as having both a responsibility and a talent and training for this management development function. There is in fact a further twist, which is that any manager who has a sizeable number of *managerial* subordinates or staff specialists will find that he or she is cast in this role. One example in the British study is a senior project manager in charge of a development team in the telecommunications industry. His subordinates consist entirely of staff professionals and middle managers – group leaders, programmers, systems analysts, designers and engineers.

Any managers with subordinates of this ilk will be involved in personnel and management development work, and it will show in a variety of ways. First, recruitment and selection assume a new importance, not just because of the level of formal qualification and expertise required but because of the importance of fitting people into a team – it is not just one more hand to drive a fork lift truck. Second, there will probably be some mechanism of periodic employee appraisal, whereby the manager has to evaluate subordinates, both for performance and potential, commit this judgment to writing and probably discuss it with the individuals concerned. But third, and probably most important, is the diffuse responsibility. Fork lift truck drivers do not confront their superiors with demands for career counselling, either metaphorically or literally, but qualified professionals and younger managers do. It is implicit in the situation that many of them are 'going somewhere' and they want to know and do the right things to go as far and as fast as is feasible.

The representative function

Textbooks about management tend to make rather a lot of the chief executive's representative function, sometimes suggesting that the top job should somehow be discharged by a small team, one of whom might concentrate on representing the company in the outside world and at ceremonial functions.[3] We suspect that the importance of the representative function is a cultural variable, that it differs from country to country, but figures large in the literature because most of the literature is American. Or perhaps it would be fairer to say that this representative function is peculiarly Anglo-Saxon, important also in Britain. Though even in Britain the pattern varies.

One British managing director we interviewed, running a plant in a small market town in the south-west, put a high premium on this representative function. The company's image in the community is vital. The town population is only 10,000 of whom half those in employment are employed by the company. So close is the integration of the company with the municipality that the company even provides an ancillary fire service for the town. In such circumstances the MD is drawn into a variety of representative and community relations roles – 'everything from Rotary to judging beauty queens'. But interestingly enough this same manager remarked that when he had earlier run a factory in the Manchester area, with a high density of managers to the square mile, the representative function had been quite insignificant.

In our experience the representative function does not amount to very much in West Germany. Top managers there seem in a certain sense shy; with one or two notable exceptions they tend to be relatively unknown to the general public, a sharp contrast with the USA, and to avoid the lime-light. Where they do mention doing things in the community it tends to be company related activities – giving talks about the company at schools or universities with a view to recruiting apprentices or young graduate employees – rather than the Anglo-Saxon mixture of Rotary and cricket matches.

In interviewing a sample of Swedish managers we found little evidence of the importance of the representative or community relations role, at least excluding more formal institutional things such as contacts with trade union headquarters or involvement in the particularly strong Swedish Employers' Federation. Indeed the only thing volunteered by a sample of chief executives was membership of the Svenska Dagbladet Club (the *Svenska Dagbladet* is a leading national newspaper, running a high status, invitation-only, visiting speakers' lunch club).

In looking at the job profile of top managers, however, it is probably also worth considering the more particular questions of relations between the company and the government or public authorities. Here again there is some national variation.

The company and government

In different ways neither Britain nor West Germany appears to be very strong cases of countries where companies seek to influence government or even have a close relationship with it. Industry has traditionally been somewhat isolated in Britain. Governments wish inflation and unemployment to go down, and growth and prosperity to go up, but do not actually seek any close relationship with industry; indeed the ideal situation would be if industry just got on with it, and delivered the goods without troubling the rest of us. In West Germany again there is something of a neutrality gap between government and industry. The dominant postwar economic doctrine in West Germany, that of the *soziale Marktwirtschaft,* actually stresses leaving market forces to flourish and keeping government interference to a minimum. Now in both countries, Britain and West Germany, government intervention has tended to increase rather than decrease with time, and to accelerate under the impact of recessionary times, but neither country is one in which close industry-government relations are seen as normal or desirable.

From the emphasis in some of the American textbooks alone one might infer a somewhat different orientation in that country, where the interests of leading companies are important to the state, and not just in a negative way (fear of shutdowns or unemployment). In the American case one can even cite examples of foreign policy initiatives which serve American business interests (almost inconceivable in Britain).

But one does not need to go as far afield as the USA for an instance of a qualitatively different relationship between industry and government, where liaison with government is a significant chief executive function. France is an excellent example.

First, anyone who studies the structure of industry in France will discover something of an organisational similarity between industry and government (or the civil service). In lay terms, a French company is simply more bureaucratic than the typical British, German or American firm. In French companies the hierarchy tends to be longer, spans of control smaller, and there are more divisions generally both functional and hierarchical — between say production and ancillary functions, between blue and white collar workers, between clerical workers and management, and so on. There is also a heavier reliance on written communication and on what we call the formal, scheduled recurrent meeting (Chapter 1) as the medium of exchange.[4]

Second, a reading of the management literature in France shows a surprising concern with unionisation (executive unionisation!), security, retirement benefits and the problem of managerial unemployment (though the rates are not higher than in comparable countries). The clue to these unexecutive yearnings may be that many French managers have actually been civil servants, and in any case civil servants and managers all come from the same stable educationally. Both senior managers (and just about all managers in big name companies) and the higher civil service are recruited from the *grandes écoles*, the 'super-universities' admitting on the basis of a competitive examination taken at the end of a two-year course *after* the completion of the French equivalent of 'A' level. From the *grandes écoles* some graduates enter industry directly, and others transfer to fairly senior positions in industry after a part-career in the higher civil service, the institution known as *pantouflage*.

The result of these overlaps and similarities is that the community of interest is greater, the exchange and mutual appreciation better. But the difference between France (and, say, Britain) is more than this. France is a country in which nationalisation (of industry) has a different meaning.[5] While in Britain nationalisation is regarded as a bit of joke, whatever the real merits, in France nationalisation means having the power of the state behind you, being an instrument of the state's desire for greater national strength, modernisation and prosperity. It is significant that, to take a popular example, Renault (nationalised) is doing well but Peugeot (private) has difficulties. But the phenomenon goes beyond the straight issue of nationalisation. The French state industrialised somewhat later than Britain, Germany and the USA, and much of this industrialisation was carried through in the post-war period. Thus it was done consciously, the development being sponsored by the state, not left to chance. The result is a qualitatively different relationship between industry and government, such as to render this liaison function a significant part of the chief executive role in France.

It may be possible to indicate the difference with a story, true of course. The head of design at a British electronics company which was a sub-contractor to the Anglo-French Concorde project described to the author the liaison meetings he used to attend in this connection. These meetings were attended by representatives of the French companies concerned and by French civil servants, and the same on the British side. What would happen, according to the English design manager, is that the French managers would gang up with their civil servants to present their case, the British civil servants would play honest broker, and the British managers would always lose.

In developing this idea of industry-government liaison as a variable component of the chief executive's role, we do not mean to make excessive capital out of the French case. France is a particularly good example, but not the only one, even in Europe. For somewhat different reasons Sweden is another country where the industry-government connection is a close one, where lobbying the government in some form or other is practically a daily habit for top managers. There are plenty of reasons for this.

First, there is the question of size. With a population of 8.3 million Sweden is a rather cosy community. This is reinforced by the fact that a great deal is concentrated in Stockholm. Practically all the major Swedish companies have their headquarters in or near Stockholm, except for Volvo at Göteborg, so that almost everyone who is anyone in business or government rubs shoulders in a town the size of Glasgow. But more important than this is the nature of the Swedish state, dominated by socialist coalitions since the 1930s and both interventionist and omnicompetent by the standards of most western countries.[6] The result is that what the state ordains is much more important for industry (has more direct effect, sets closer boundaries, may offer more help) than in, say, Britain or West Germany. Let us offer a simple example.

Since the start of the 1980 recession it has become clear that there is a world over-capacity in alcoholic drinks. This is especially true for breweries. Everyone is trying to export beer to everyone else; the fate of a European brewery may hang on its success or failure in penetrating the vast north American market (current leader with an estimated 10 per cent stake, Heineken). Now it just so happens that Denmark has banned beer cans on environmentalist grounds. But this in effect protects Denmark from beer imports since it is impractical to move beer over long distances in anything except cans. Sweden, of course, would have claim to being the most environmentally conscious country in the world, and the government is rumoured to be considering a Danish-style ban. Would this be worth lobbying for?

In suggesting some of the characteristic concerns of chief executives we have tried to go a little beyond the obvious facts of ultimate responsibility for policy and financial performance, and in doing so we have made liberal use of examples from other countries. We will conclude with a brief consideration of the characteristic responsibilities of senior production managers. The subjects of this final discussion do not necessarily enjoy the title 'director' (see Chapter 1) although most do; it is rather a question of their representing the highest level of responsibility for production whatever the individual's formal rank.

Policy makers in production or the role of the works director

To some extent this is an exercise in re-statement since many of the concerns of production bosses have been indicated in earlier itemisations of problems or in examples of the content of various kinds of meeting. It may still help to put the distinctive essentials under four headings.

Personnel

There is a complex of personnel decisions and activities. First, there is the question already discussed in connection with the role of higher managers, that of the personal development of managerial subordinates in career terms, and occasional promotion decisions. Second, there is the formal matter of ratifying promotions, transfers, appointments and demotions lower down in the production empire. Third, there are industrial relations decisions, usually in the form of occasionally intervening watch-dog and big stick waver rather than of regular involvement in the details. Third, and related to this, it is usual in our experience for worker representative committees of the type described in Chapter 2 to be chaired by a senior production manager (rather than by a personnel manager). The production boss also has an ultimate responsibility for deciding on the overall size and composition of the (production) workforce, and will be required to sanction significant changes in its deployment (e.g. introduction of shiftwork, transfers between plants). Similarly, the production boss will bear responsibility for, and may actually personally pass on to the workforce, unpalatable decisions and news — closures, phased redundancies, rundown, reductions of head-count (a standard euphemism for getting rid of people), non-replacement policies and rationalisation (rationalisation is seldom good news).

Decisions with money implications

There are a bundle of decisions with cost and expenditure implications which are the responsibility of senior production managers. The most obvious is bearing the ultimate responsibility for debts and obligations which production has contracted, and, as we have seen, for pressurising the finance department to pay debts so as to enforce continued supplies. The production boss may, or may not, have responsibility for choosing suppliers, or ratifying the choice. Sometimes the purchasing function is in a formal organisational sense under the control of production (Chapter 1) and sometimes it is not. And again, depending on the nature of the product, its technical sophistication and degree of customisation (the extent to which it is adapted for individual customers), supplier decisions may be made by designers or engineers, rather than by production or purchasing departments (Chapter 3).

Another variable responsibility is the involvement of production in pricing policy (setting the prices for the company's products, either in general or for particular customers). Sometimes this is a top management decision, sometimes a marketing decision and sometimes a production decision; there are of course various 'mixes' of price decision-taking as well. Finally there is the question of capital expenditure decisions for the acquisition of new plant and equipment. In Britain these are usually initiated by a production engineering department rather than by production itself, and production engineers are more likely to choose what to buy than are line production managers. The fact remains, however, that such expenditure decisions are usually the responsibility of a senior production manager, and are charged *to* production whoever makes them. In German companies production managers themselves tend to be more involved in the initiation and choice, as well as bearing the budgetary responsibility.

Interface responsibility

Production bosses bear a rather heavy responsibility for managing the interface between production and the numerous other departments and functions upon which it depends. Though this point requires little elaboration here in view of the examples given in previous chapters, especially Chapters 2, 3, and 6.

Reporting to the chief executive

Finally the production boss will report to the managing director or other on-site chief executive. This is true by definition for all the functional heads but it often has a special significance in the case of production. This is that the production boss is especially vulnerable in this respect since his empire is large, multifarious, and highly visible (whereas the typical managing director will only have a vague idea what is going on in say R & D or in the management services department). Fussy managing directors, and there are plenty of them, may well use the production boss as a whipping boy for everything that displeases them from intractable shop stewards to empty crisp packets in the car park. This is in addition to the production manager's more formal accountability!

Returning for a moment to the theme explored in Chapters 1 and 2, the allocation of time between various types of activity, it is again possible to characterise the work pattern of the senior production manager. He will spend more time in formal meetings, and chair more of them; spend more time on desk work, travel more and spend much less time in tours of the works.

Summary

The previous chapter looked at the characteristic problems faced by production managers and general managers in charge of production units, and considered the decisions made to solve these. The present chapter is a companion piece thereto, seeking to describe the concerns and preoccupations of chief executives and heads of major divisions. In offering this account we have tended to take the obvious as read and to consider some of the less tangible and programmable aspects of the chief executive role. In this connection we have considered, and in most cases given examples of, the question of acquisition of other companies, the issue of top manager succession, the responsibility for building up the business, divining new applications for existing products or services, the role of analysis in the direction of companies, personnel and industrial relations decisions, the representative function and relations between industry and government. Finally we considered the distinctive features of the role of the production boss, and noted ways in which his work pattern differs from that of production managers in general.

Notes

1 This idea of control without ownership is propounded in K.J. Blois, 'Vertical Quasi-Integration', *The Journal of Industrial Economics*, vol. XX, July 1973, no. 3.
2 The importance of social-political skills for top managers in Britain is clear in the account of a survey, Charles Margerison, 'How Chief Executives Succeed', *Human Resource Development*, vol. 4, no. 9, 1980.
3 The importance of the representative function is pressed, for example, in Ernest Dale, *Management Theory and Practice*, McGraw-Hill, New York, 1965.

4   For a summary in English of recent research which suggests the bureau-
    cratic nature of French companies see S.P. Hutton, P.A. Lawrence and
    J.H. Smith, 'The Recruitment, Deployment, and Status of the Mechanical
    Engineer in the German Federal Republic', Report to the Department
    of Industry, London, 1977 (also available from the University of
    Loughborough library). The discussion of French companies is in vol. 1,
    section 6.
5   The idea of the different meaning of nationalisation in France is
    developed in Peter Lawrence, 'Business Vitality and Bureaucracy in
    France', *The Business Graduate*, Summer 1981.
6   A comprehensive if rather unsympathetic account of the pervasive
 · power of the Swedish state is offered in Roland Huntford, *The New
    Totalitarians*, Allen Lane, 1971.

Further reading

Two of the books listed at the end of Chapter 2 deal very much with the
work and concerns of top managers:

SUNE CARLSON, *Executive Behaviour*, Strombergs, Stockholm, 1951.
HENRY MINTZBERG, *The Nature of Managerial Work*, Harper & Row, New
York, 1973.

For a different perspective on how companies should 'organise for victory'
see ROBERT HELLER, *The Business of Winning*, Sidgwick & Jackson,
1980.

A broader account of industry and management in Sweden, from which
country several of the top manager examples in Chapter 7 are taken, is
given in PETER LAWRENCE, 'Swedish Management: Context and Character',
Report to the Social Science Research Council, London, December 1982
(also available from the University of Loughborough library).

Top management responsibility points into the fashionable area of business policy; for a lucid introduction see the chapter by Gerry Johnson on
business policy in C.K. ELLIOTT and P.A. LAWRENCE (eds), *Introducing
Management*, Penguin, 1984.

Discussion questions

1 What is the operational case for quasi-vertical integration? Is there any way in which it is open to abuse?
2 How would you go about picking people to run manufacturing subsidiaries abroad of a British based food processing company? Take as test cases subsidiaries located in Mexico, Switzerland and Australia.
3 Attempt a job description for the post of works director to be appointed from outside, to a medium-sized mechanical engineering company.
4 In what ways is top management engaged in 'people work'?
5 Imagine you have become head of an electric vacuum cleaner company in Britain that is losing market share and profitability. What sort of measures might affect a 'turn-round'?

8

The company and
the environment

Any company is tied in to its environment in a lot of different ways. Many of these ways are obvious, and practical examples have occurred in previous chapters. On the other hand, the more pervasive effects and constraints that the environing society has on a business organisation are less obvious, and national differences in such effects have only come to light in research studies of the last few years. It may be helpful to start with a practical illustration from one of the English case studies, and show how some 'purely internal matters' have implications for the relationship between the company and its environment.

The managing director's weekly meeting

At this small food processing plant in south-west England with some 385 employees the managing director holds a general purpose meeting at 10 a.m. each Monday. This company, although small, is part of a foreign owned multi-national, which fact is reflected in some of the issues discussed:

1 The MD welcomes a newly appointed supervisor to the meeting. He goes on to announce that some visitors from another factory in the group will be arriving – the purpose of their visit is to study the way tin cans (for the produce) are made, with a view to establishing a canning line in their own factory in Scotland; the visit of an engineering specialist from the European headquarters is announced – he is coming to investigate some particular technical malfunction; and the impending arrival of a group of engineers from the British head office is announced – they are going to mastermind the installation of a new and very important piece of equipment.

2 The engineering manager announces that an incinerator they are buying from an outside supplier is on the way, and the boiler for it has already arrived. The MD intervenes to ask how long it will be before the whole lot is installed and functioning.

3 The production manager reports that two loads of a powder-form raw material have been 'lost' between the docks and the factory – the suggestion is that the private haulage company is to blame. This engenders further discussion of such material losses, and it emerges that another consignment froze and deteriorated while being held at the docks.

4 The administration manager announces that the new telex installed the previous Friday (it is a bigger and better version of their old telex machine) will come 'on stream' shortly with the post office running a user training scheme the following afternoon.

5 The manager in charge of the tin shop where the cans are made gives a talk on the work of his section and operating changes expected in the coming year. These changes include some retooling to make cans of a new size on an existing line, some technical improvements in fabrication, a better matching of the needs of the production section with a consequent reduction of buffer stocks. The only thing they have not managed to do is to talk the Marketing Department (at head office) into doing away with two different tin sizes for one particular product. The personnel manager takes up the personnel implications of these intended changes in the tin shop, and it is agreed that new employees should be taken on, but not how many.

Dependence on the environment

The five points listed above represent a summary of a forty-two-minute meeting run by a managing director with all his subordinates of super-visory rank or above. We would like to suggest that these few items, although they all appear to be straightforwardly concerned with manu-facturing exigencies, highlight at several points the dependence of the company on the environment.

First, the installation of the improved telex facility is a reminder of the dependence of a company on contacts with the rest of the world, on a need for written communications faster than normal mail. Second, the MD's announcements at the beginning make it clear that companies do actually have visitors, and not simply in the person of prospective cus-tomers. Third, the reference to the purchase and installation of the incinerator points up the very substantial dependence of most companies on outside sources of materials and equipment: a consideration which has come up in several connections, and particularly in the discussion of delivery punctuality (Chapter 5). Fourth, the dependence of most com-panies on the national transport system of the country in which they are located comes out, and not for the first time in the examples presented is the fact that in Britain one cannot take good service at the docks for granted. Fifth is the related point that the company in question here, like the majority, is also dependent on others for road haulage, and that this is held to pose its problems as well. Sixth, the planned changes in tin production indicate a need for extra employees: in fact this was unlikely to be a problem for a company located in a predominantly rural area, but this fact together with the widespread unemployment of the 1980s should not lead one to take for granted the availability of manpower. All but one of the German firms the author has ever visited had contingents of south European workers, a testimony to labour shortages in West Germany in the 1960s and 1970s. Furthermore, British firms in the case study sample variously indicated shortages of maintenance fitters, instrument artificers, electronics graduates, welders and programmers in a period reaching into the 1980s recession.

The discussion in the meeting concerning the desirability of having tins of one size only for a particular product is also instructive for the way the environment impinges on a company. Internal logistics suggest simplifying by having a single size, but marketing specialists at the UK head office insist on the product being available in different sized packages. This is almost certainly a market research based decision, and as such is a nice example of the general public giving a company an operating problem.

The talk given by the manager in charge of the tin shop has a secondary significance. The task was a prepared set piece, and it is the policy of the MD to have various subordinates talk about their work and expected developments in their departments, as much as a personal development exercise as for the information imparted. Now this is a perfectly reasonable thing to do, but it is also very English culture-bound, along the lines of prefects saying grace and the third form taking it in turn to read in assembly.

Yet perhaps the most important environmental reference in the MD's meeting is to the existence and impingement of the rest of the company on this particular firm in the form of visitors and specialists from other parts of the empire.

Head Office as environment

In setting the company scene in Chapter 1 it was suggested that most manufacturing companies do not 'stand alone' but are part of some larger corporate entity. The food processing company discussed above is a very strong example of this phenomenon, and there are several allusions to its multi-national status in the managing director's meeting. It would be possible to go further and say that the most important part of the environment for most companies is their own head office.

The hostility with which head office is often viewed has come up several times in practical illustrations but it may be helpful to draw the strands together and say for what reasons and on what counts the head office is so often resented.

Arguing from the range of works versus head office resentments which have emerged in the study in companies in both Britain and Germany, it would seem that they fall under four general headings.

1 *Money* Head offices control funds. They exercise a higher order budgetary control, decide on the extent to which member firms may retain profits, make financial allocatory decisions among firms in the group, and often approve (and fund) capital expenditure initiatives of individual works in the group. All this is enough to guarantee that the typical head office makes a lot of money decisions which offend people at works level. To give a homely example, one of the British companies had a very pressing operational need for new packaging machinery. The existing machinery broke down frequently with a disruptive effect on distribution. The head office would not approve expenditure on the new machinery, and muddied the local pool even more by justifying the refusal on the grounds that a forthcoming re-distribution of the various products between several constituent firms would render the packaging machinery redundant (meanwhile they could put up with the breakdowns). But what further inflamed local passions was the head office decision to spend vastly more money up-grading all the laboratories in the firms in the group. This leads to the second consideration.

2 *Policy decisions* Head offices take policy decisions which have general application (to various parts of the corporate group). However well-founded and well-conceived such decisions may be, there will always be some part of the group ready to claim that it is not really appropriate to them to do whatever it is. Indeed the whole head office policy making role is open to the subfused objection that the policy makers are too far from the coal face to stand much chance of getting it right. Just to take one example from the study of a head office decision which caused local resentment, the head office concerned announced a policy of graduates only for the top positions in the various works to bring the UK management structure into line with that abroad. At this time many of the second positions at the works were filled by non-graduates who had confidently

expected to get to the top in time.

3 *Demands for information* If there is one thing for which head office can be depended on it is to demand a steady stream of information from the constituent companies. Much of this is standardised, recurrent and predictable, such as the uniform budgetary controls, financial reporting and auditing activities. But the head office also has a knack of asking for information on an inspirational basis: data on the structure of the work-force, age of workforce by section, quarterly consumption of kwh of electricity per direct worker, expenditure on car park maintenance, number of automatic drinks machines per 1,000 of workforce, or propor-tion of managers under 35 enrolled for the Diploma of Management Studies (DMS) course. These one-off or at least unscheduled demands for information tend to be unpalatable to the constituent companies in two ways. First, the company yielding up the information is never quite sure to what use the head office will put it – but fears the worst (see next section). Second, actually collecting this information is pure hassle – who wants to count the drinks machines, or spend an afternoon fooling around with the last five years' electricity bills – and when the information collecting job has been done those who have done it have to make up the lost time on their 'real work'.

4 *Head office and bureaucratic rationality* Head office personnel tend to perceive themselves as a force for rationality and efficiency, and the promotion of these ends may involve the initiation of constructive change. At works level, head office personnel are seen as force for bureaucracy, standardisation and administrative nit-picking, and if there is one thing that is feared above all else it is constructive change initiated by someone else.

In particular it is understood that head office will react to anomalies in the empire, which is at least pseudo-rational because in theory there ought to be one best way to do it and if the company has found it the same arrangements should prevail from Maidstone to Manchester. This is why the yielding up of recherché information is feared: today you provide some data as requested, tomorrow an unsuspecting works manager in darkest Doncaster will be rapped over the knuckles from London (Brussels or New Jersey) because too few of his subordinates are enrolled on the DMS course, or the number of reserved parking lots is dispropor-tionally high by group standards.

Head office: expertise and support

The line of argument advanced in the previous section is true but incomplete of course. What head office is valued for is being a repository of helpful specialised knowledge which individual works need on occasion but cannot provide from their own resources. To put it another way, constituent companies implicitly distinguish between operational independence and problem solving. Head office demands, rulings, and above all personal visitation which constrain the operating independence of managers at works level are resented, but help in solving problems which threaten smooth operations is welcomed.

Our impression is that the positive valuation of head office support and expertise is patterned according to the sophistication of the product, and even more of the process. The companies in both Britain and Germany where head office support was praised at works level were in the chemical industry and food processing industry in particular. In other words, where routine operations depend on sophisticated inputs of knowledge, equipment, or process design, head office has most to give.

A food processing company in Germany offered a quite dramatic demonstration of this thesis. The company had been experiencing a middle-term quality problem centring on the degeneration of the critical raw material at a particular point in the process. The West German head office sent its specialist who was received in the conference room by all the interested parties headed by the works director. The specialist swaggered in like the German officer in a war film, demanded the assembled throng to explain their reasoning and experimentation to date, then produced an explanatory hypothesis of his own. He devised instant tests to check the hypothesis, and carried them out in public in the conference room, with senior managers carrying his test tubes for him. The test invalidated the hypothesis. Undismayed he produced a new explanatory hypothesis, more tests, hypothesis-proved, free-hand drawings on the blackboard to show the peasants what it was all about, a quick word with the works engineer to tell him what bit of preventive equipment to install, and back to head office in his Jaguar. An hour and a half for a problem they had been wrestling with for weeks.

A similar if less dramatic transaction occurred at the English food processing company where the managing director's weekly meeting has been used to illustrate various propositions about a company's dependence on its environment. On the afternoon following the MD's meeting, head office specialists got together with all the interested parties from the works to discuss the installation and testing of important new equipment. This meeting, chaired by the works MD, is an ideal example of both the positive dependency and the tensions between head office and works.

The meeting began with a statement from the host MD that the headquarters team was only there to advise, and that the works have real responsibility. The point of this remark can only be political – a warning shot, just to remind these head office impresarios that they'll be gone tomorrow but we will be running the plant. It was not very convincing in fact because as the meeting progressed a marked disparity in relevant knowledge became clear.

The works people had no idea about the new equipment. They knew how to run such equipment in routine operating terms and that is all. The head office specialists actually knew how and why it worked, but more than this they did not only have science-knowledge of it but had experience in installing it, testing it and de-bugging it at other plants around the world. Their appreciation of all that was involved was quite masterful.

At the same time there was a fatuous element in the headquarters visitation. The meeting was on a Tuesday afternoon, it was agreed that the equipment should be test run for a couple of days, and then the works production manager suggested the group should reconvene on Friday to discuss the test results. But Friday did not please the head office team: too near the weekend and they are 200 miles from London. They grudgingly agree to shorten the test run and have the meeting on Thursday afternoon 'as long as we start promptly at 2 p.m.' Then the leader of the HQ team was asked when he would next come down among them, a relevant question since what was planned was a series of test runs and monitorings before the equipment became fully operational in the following month. He did not know, his first loyalty he said was to another plant in East Anglia also undergoing technical up-dating. But if he could not see it through, why had he come?

The primacy of the economic environment

Companies tend to define the extra corporate environment primarily in economic terms, which comes out in a number of ways:

Suppliers

The previous reference to suppliers and their role in determining the delivery performance of a company have been in terms of the availability and reliability of suppliers. It should be emphasised here, however, that for the typical company the price structure of the various suppliers is an important part of that company's economic environment. The typical company spends more on paying for materials and bought-out-parts than it does on the labour bill; and the cost of bought-out-parts runs at around 60 per cent of all manufacturing costs (including wages and overheads) in both Britain and the USA.[1] When a supplier announces a price rise, this may be very bad news for companies at the receiving end of it. Similarly especially large companies are increasingly using their clout to get better deals from suppliers.[2]

Furthermore companies quite often come into conflict with their suppliers about money. When the supplier sends the wrong item, and it has to be replaced, who pays for it? When the supplier sends defective components, and rather than sustain the delay of sending them back the receiving company does some rectification work on them itself, how does it get the supplier to pay? Sometimes such disagreements lead to litigation. In one of the German companies in the study insulating material had been obtained from an American company, used to insulate the German company's products, and been thus installed in the premises of a number of customers. The insulation proved defective, the German company had to make amends to some of its customers, and at the time of the study was in the process of suing the supplier on the grounds that the supplier's promotional literature claimed the insulating material was suitable for exactly the purpose to which they had put it. The German company initiating the litigation had also prepared the ground by having lab tests of the material made by a third party which highlighted the material's shortcomings.

Price wars

A highly significant part of the environment of many companies is what rival companies are doing, a fact that has come up in some of the previous illustrations (for example the new design special purpose meeting at the German equipment company described in Chapter 2). The most common form of interaction between rival companies is, of course, price competition. In fact price war is a normal state of affairs for many companies.

Breweries, for instance, in all the western countries are in sharp competition with each other. The price structure which any one brewery adopts will be significantly constrained by what the competition are doing. The only way to break out of this competition, at least in the short run until others catch up, is to bring out something new, or newly packaged, or oriented to a putative newly perceived need. An example in the drinks industry is the appearance of three- and four-litre refrigerated wine boxes: they have novelty appeal, and they satisfy a continuity-availability need, but are patently over-priced in that one can get a better deal by volume through buying three or four conventional one-litre bottles.

An example of really sophisticated price competition is offered by the oil companies, especially in their dealings with industrial or institutional customers. The price of oil fluctuates short term so that in the first instance oil companies are competing in terms of spot price ('buy ours, we're cheapest on Tuesday!'). But customers also understand about these short-term fluctuations, so in the second place oil companies are competing in terms of their price record over a period. So that an oil company salesman may argue that his company has never been more than 5 per cent away from the mean price in the last year, or better still, has kept its prices within the margin of 2 per cent above and 5 per cent below the mean price. What is more, the stable and continual price competition may provoke a reaction in the sense that since none of the contenders is likely to be able to win the price war outright, individual companies may seek to differentiate their offering in some other way while continuing to play the price war game. One of the 'seven sisters' oil companies, for example, managed to maintain a high level of continuity of supply to its industrial customers in Britain in the 1973-4 oil shortages: this established reputation for reliability is still used by the company's salesmen.[3]

In other cases price competition is spasmodic and tactical. At a works committee meeting of the type described in Chapter 2 a British manufacturing director was pressed by worker representatives to explain the company's declining profitability (and anticipated poor pay offer). The manufacturing director replied in terms of rising material and operating costs (it is an energy intensive and highly equipped plant). But surely material and operating costs have risen before, reply the workers' representatives, so what else is going on? All right, concedes the manufacturing director, what we usually do is put the price up, but this time we're pegged by a rival firm trying to undercut us and take our market share.

Sometimes these price wars assume a combative and personalised form. One British company we know supplies an industrial product to a range of user industries. Traditionally it has dealt in the top market, selling to large and medium-sized firms, but is now trying to break into the small industrial user market as well. Unfortunately the small user market is dominated by a very successful though smaller rival, on whom war has now been declared. The marketing executive in charge of the sales task force expressed their mission as: 'What we want is to get him (MD of rival company) out of his Rolls Royce with radio telephone, and into a Ford Sierra with a CB.'

Take-overs

An important part of any company's economic environment is any capacity or initiative 'out there' to buy you up. In the discussion of acquisitions in Chapter 7 we argued there are really two types, strategic and opportunistic, and that the opportunistic type are the most threatening. A strategic acquisition to obtain a source of supply or a distribution facility is to some extent predictable. Companies know, after all, who their customers are and who could benefit by acquiring them. It is also possible that strategic acquisitions have run their course for the time being, and large companies are in any case coming to recognise the merits of quasi-vertical integration, or control without ownership. But opportunistic take-overs may come from any direction at any time, and business folk-lore does not provide a preventive move. Companies which do badly are in principle vulnerable because the take-over company may be able to turn them round with share value and profitability gains. On the other hand companies which do well are also vulnerable: if they are making good profits others will want to enjoy them. Enormous size is one barrier, and it has been suggested by a French executive that rapid and sustained growth is another.[4]

When take-overs occur there are usually a lot of after-effects for those at the receiving end: the assuaging message that is sometimes put out at the time of a take-over that it will change nothing except the ownership of the company is seldom true. Typically a take-over will be followed by key personnel changes, by new control systems, a torrent of information requests from head office, and often a general tightening up. A good example of some of these features is the German brewery described in Chapter 6 where the incoming production director followed a programme of general tightening up including cost cutting, disciplining foremen and others, raising quality standards and introducing new process control technology — and he experienced some personal resentments. It is also of interest that this company had appointed a small committee to redesign the organisation's formal structure (see Chapter 6).

Business competitions

In Britain at any rate there has been a new and interesting response to the economic environment by some large and successful firms. The response has been an attempt to better a rather sluggish economic climate and to stimulate the provision of industrial employment, usually in particular regions. The means adopted by benefactor companies have been business competitions providing the winners with venture capital, or interest free loans, or low interest loans, or subsidised premises, or free consultancy services or some mixture of all of these. In the late 1970s Shell pioneered the Enterprise North scheme in conjunction with the Durham University Business School and a consortium of northern businessmen; the scheme offered cash prizes and other assistance to the winners to set up new businesses in the area or to expand or transfer-in existing businesses.

In the spring of 1980 Pilkington Brothers, the famous glassworks in St Helens, announced the creation of the Rainford Venture Capital Trust whose function again was to pick would-be or existing entrepreneurs who need start-up or expansion capital. The Pilkington approach has been a little different in that the scheme is a rolling one, there is no deadline or batching of applicants, and the philosophy has been to make a small number of large awards. In other words the Pilkington initiative does not aim at sustaining small businesses as an end in itself, but at trying to create a few big businesses in the long term.

Another regional initiative has come from Pedigree Petfoods in Melton Mowbray, a company belonging to the Mars Group. They ran business competitions in conjunction with various local authorities and with the support of the Small Business Unit at Loughborough University in both 1982 and 1983. Again the winners received cash prizes, reduced rate premises, low interest loans and free consultancy.

To end with a speculative observation, we would expect big company initiatives of this kind to proliferate, indeed there may come a time when they are a near standard part of the corporate response to the economic environment. The reasoning is that unemployment is likely to stay undesirably high for years even if there is some improvement; and that in this climate some of the big companies which do well will do so in part through rationalisation and an increasingly productive technology (and a smaller work force). If there is one thing we can learn from nineteenth-century English history it is that wealth crossed with guilt is a powerful spur to charity.

Culture's consequence and the Anglo-German comparison

In discussing some features of the top manager's role in Chapter 7 reference was made to the need to liaise with government and public authorities, a need which seems to vary from country to country but is strong in France. In the same connection, the idea that there are marked similarities between the structure and *modus operandi* of French companies and that of the French state was developed. As a final thrust we would like to take the argument a stage further and suggest that among the intangible yet important effects of the environment on the business firm is the conditioning effect of the total national culture. This argument can be pursued in terms of the Anglo-German comparison, which will also bring together strands of a sub-theme of the book.

At several points already attention has been drawn to interesting differences between industry and management in Great Britain and West Germany. The distribution of time between the various types of activity propounded in the first chapter differs for managers in the two countries, with the British managers quite simply spending a higher proportion of time in formal meetings. It is not clear from the figures given in Chapter 1 because of different conventions in classifying activity as between the British and German samples but another activity difference is that the Germans spent a higher proportion of time touring the works and on the shop floor. There are differences in the qualificational profile for managers in the two countries, and for that matter for foremen. The status relativities among the areas of management work differ, as does the overall salience of status issues. The personnel function is very different in the German context, and the two countries show a marked difference in level of industrial relations activity. Furthermore they have different records and reputations on the question of delivery punctuality. It is possible to re-group these identified differences, and enlarge on them, in the context of four general propositions.

Finance versus Technik

British industry has a marked financial orientation. It is strongly oriented to 'profits now' (or as soon as we can get at them). It emphasises financial control and budgetary surveillance, and accountants play an important part in the British system. Expenditure is closely controlled, and expenditure decisions strongly linked to hierarchical status. Capital expenditure is not a priority, and there is little enthusiasm for expenditure on activities which do not contribute directly to profit (such as maintenance).

None of this is entirely absent in German companies, of course, but the emphasis is less. In Germany there is a much stronger technical orientation. The technical functions in a German company tend to have higher relative standing, and managers tend to be better qualified on the technical side than their colleagues on the commercial side. The things which are considered most important in Germany are design, manufacturing methods and the perfectability of products. Status, and to a lesser extent remuneration and promotion chances, follows these lines.

When British managers are asked what they are proud of they tend to answer in commercial terms with references to profitability, cost-reduction, growth of turnover or of market share. Germans answer with references to productivity, delivery, methods and above all the presumptive quality of products. British managers think industry is about making money: Germans that it is about making three-dimensional artifacts.

The British are more managerial

It is one of the peculiarities of comparative philology that the Germans do not have an indigenous word for manager (though they do for entrepreneur). British industry is much more managerially oriented, and it comes out in several ways. The British are much more strongly attached to the idea of management, as a universal entity about which general propositions can be made. And like the Americans they are believers in the virtue of explicitly managerial training. The British, indeed, are much more strongly Americanised than the Germans, and for at least the first thirty years after the Second World War took the USA as the obvious mentor in business matters.

The British emphasise the generalist approach to management, and a British manager is proud to call himself 'a good all-rounder'. There is a corresponding emphasis on variety of experience − between functions, between companies, and even between industries. The British are more interested in 'the human side of enterprise', and have more to say both personally and in the literature about communication and motivation. Personality considerations and especially social skills are more important in choosing, and advancing, managers in Britain.

Again none of this is absent in Germany but there are differences of degree and emphasis. The predominant orientations there are technical and specialist. German managers are qualified in engineering, business economics and law, not in business administration. Indeed there are no

Anglo-American style business schools in West Germany, no MBAs, and no undergraduate courses in business administration.

Germans are neurotic

In the earlier discussion of the performance of the two countries on delivery punctuality (Chapter 5) reference was made to a cross-cultural study suggesting that there is a strain of neuroticism among Germans. One might re-formulate this more politely by saying that Germans, at least many German managers, have a striving, perfectionist, achievement-oriented persona which perhaps has a neurotic underpinning. This characterises German management in some measure and differentiates it. As suggested earlier, this managerial personality leads to a concern with products, deadlines and general perfectionism. It leads to caution and planning, and always having something in reserve. It militates against virtuosity in fire-fighting and instant managerial resourcefulness: these are British strengths.

German management is the product of society

Finally it is our view that German management is much more positively shaped by other institutions and values of German society. To start with, the whole idea of *Technik*, of the lustre of engineering and the fascination of making things, belongs to German society as a whole – industry is simply the exemplar and beneficiary. Second, various forces in German society have combined to give industry a high status, and higher than it has traditionally been in the UK. Again German industry has been the beneficiary of this, especially in terms of being a strong career choice for able and well-qualified people. Third, this status of industry is sustained in Germany by a materialism which is much more explicit than in Britain, and by a general public concern with economic achievement as a national as well as personal phenomenon. This derives no doubt from the economic rigours of the immediate post-war period, and from the fact that in the post-1945 world, economic achievement was the only form of achievement open to the Germans. Fourth, German management exemplifies the national predilection for specialism rather than generalism. German culture valorises specialised knowledge and competence, and this dominates thinking about work. The practical effect of this for industry is that the managerial qualification profile is somewhat higher, and that German industry is, at least numerically, swamped by engineers. Foremen are more likely to have had formal training, and apprenticeship training is both taken more seriously and available for a wider range of job specialisms, including production as well as maintenance-fitter trades as in Britain. German managers are more likely to give their occupation as designer, production controller or salesman rather than say they are managers. Finally, there is not only a closer connection in Germany between what people study and the work they do afterwards, entirely in line with the specialist orientation, but also more rapport and mutual esteem between industry and the world of formal education.

This idea of national culture as a partial determinant of the character of management which has been propounded here with reference to the Anglo-German comparison is relatively new. But the next stage is already in train, one which in effect concerns itself with transfers and transplantations. This second stage seeks to answer questions such as: do American firms in Britain retain a distinctively American character (and what is it), will British firms in Germany remain British or be Germanised, can the virtues of Japanese management (whatever they are) be transplanted to other countries?

Summary

This chapter has been concerned with the relationship between business firms and the overall environment, taking as a *point de départ* the issues raised in a routine meeting in a British company in the study. The idea that the head office in particular is an important part of the environment of any constituent company was developed, with some analysis of both the support and provocation with which the typical head office confronts its works. Next the idea of the primacy of the economic environment was discussed with particular reference to financial relations with suppliers, price wars, take-overs and the emergent institution of the business competition.

Finally we took up the idea of the national culture as a determining variable for the character of management in different countries, and illustrated this in terms of a comparison between management in Britain and West Germany. The next objective in comparative management research will be to discover how far, and under what conditions, the managerial strengths of one country can be transplanted to others.

Notes

1   The importance of the purchasing function and the cost of bought out parts is demonstrated in Brian Farrington and Michael Woodmansey, 'The Purchasing Function', Management Survey Report no. 50, British Institute of Management, 1980.

2   For an account of how big companies exploit their purchasing power see P.A. Lawrence and R.A. Lee, *Insight into Management*, Oxford University Press, 1984.

3   This idea of price competition and the way it is handled by salesmen is discussed in Peter Lawrence and John Mansfield, 'The Relativity of the Marketing Mix' in Proceedings of the Marketing Education Group conference, Cranfield Institute of Technology, July 1983.

4   The notion that only rapid growth can protect a company against take-over is suggested in an interview with a French entrepreneur in Roger Priouret, *Les Managers Européens*, Denoel, Paris, 1970.

Further reading

On American companies in Britain, and whether they are really different, see IAN JAMIESON, *Capitalism and Culture: A Comparative Analysis of British and American Manufacturing Organisations*, Gower, 1980.

Among the best of the many recent books on Japanese management, and in particular Japanese companies in Britain, is MICHAEL WHITE and MALCOLM TREVOR, *Under Japanese Management*, Heinemann, 1983.

For a discussion of business competitions and small firms see PETER LAWRENCE (ed.), *Small Business Breakthrough*, Martin Robertson, 1985.

On the general question of the effects of national culture on business practice and organisational structure see C.J. LAMMERS (ed.), *Organisations Alike and Unlike*, Routledge & Kegan Paul, 1979.

Discussion questions

1   Analyse the tensions and dependencies that exist between head office and constituent companies.

2   What does it mean to say that the environment of a company is primarily economic?

3 In what ways does price link companies to the environment?
4 How would you judge entrants in a business competition for venture capital money?
5 Consider any of the management meetings detailed in Chapter 2 as evidence for the dictum 'the environment pervades company operations in all details'.

Index

147

Printed in the United States
by Baker & Taylor Publisher Services